PRAYING
THE
PSALMS

EXPERIENCING
SCRIPTURE-FED
SPIRIT-LED
WORSHIP-BASED PRAYER

Volume 2   Psalms 42–72

Daniel Henderson
General Editor

6:4PRESS

Praying the Psalms: Experiencing Scripture-Fed, Spirit-Led, Worship-Based Prayer
Volume 2 (43 - 72)

Library of Congress Cataloging-in-Publication Data

ISBN: 978-0-9816090-7-2

To learn more about 6:4PRESS publishing opportunities, contact: info@strategicrenewal.com

Publishing services provided by Fitting Words LLC. www.fittingwords.net

OTHER BOOKS IN THE
PRAYING THE PSALMS SERIES

Praying the Psalms Volume 1 (Psalms 1–41)

TABLE OF CONTENTS

PREFACE

F or almost two decades I met with a small group of faithful church members every Sunday morning, typically at 6:30 a.m. Each week we would read a psalm at the outset of our gathering. We would reflect on the truths we observed about God and His character. Then, uniting prayers of praise and spontaneous song, we would spend the next 20 minutes worshipping from the Word of God.

After a few moments of quiet surrender to the will and kingdom concerns of our Father, we would disperse throughout the church campus, praying with heartfelt requests for the needs of the day. Some would prayer walk in the area of the children's ministry, others would intercede for the youth in their section of the campus. Some would remain in the auditorium, walking among the rows, praying for receptive hearts during the upcoming service. I would often pray in the area of the choir loft and, of course, the pulpit.

At a designated time, we would re-gather in the front of the worship center as these faithful intercessors gathered around the worship pastor and me, asking for the Lord's favor on our leadership of the services. I often noted that the two of us were no more important in that moment, just more desperate.

Over the years, we went through the Psalms five times, simply praying from the next psalm each week. I can testify that I learned how to pray in those weekly gatherings. Those 60-minute prayer experiences each Sunday ministered to my soul and prepared me to preach in ways that I still cannot fully articulate. It seemed that each psalm was perfectly timed for the needs of the day and fueled our prayers of faith for the work of the Lord.

We would interact with each psalm through the lens of the model prayer commanded by Jesus in Matthew 6:9-13 and Luke 11:2-4. The beautiful convergence of the truths in each psalm with the rhythm of prayer taught by Christ was fresh and instructive every Sunday.

This guide will invite you to also experience the power of praying the Psalms, just as we did over those many years. I pray you will fully maximize this resource personally, in your family, and even in your church or broader ministry endeavors. I believe it will show you fresh pathways of transforming prayer.

Dietrich Bonhoeffer stated that "The Psalter is the great school of prayer" and that "We learn from the prayer of the Psalms what we should pray."[1] So, enter in to this school of prayer. Learn to pray more biblically, more honestly, and more faithfully.

Not long ago, I posted this thought on social media: "The great privilege of prayer is to open your Bible to experience a conversation with the Author who lives in you to explain what He meant by what He said and then inspire your heart to apply that truth in an intimate engagement that will transform your life –and empower you as an agent of gospel transformation in the world."

The author of the Psalms, ultimately the Holy Spirit, awaits your pursuit of the Lord in prayer. He will illumine, guide, comfort, convict, and change you. I truly pray your journey through the Psalms in prayer will do as much for you as it has done for me – and even more.

For His glory,

Daniel Henderson
Founder and President of Strategic Renewal
Global Director, *The 6:4 Fellowship*

---

[1] Dietrich Bonhoeffer, *Life Together: The Classic Exploration of Christian Community* (New York: Harper & Row, 1954), 47.

A CALL TO CORPORATE PRAYER
Pray alone or with others?

People often ask, "Which is more important, private prayer or corporate prayer?" Our answer is a resounding, "Yes!" This is like asking which leg do we need to walk, the right or the left. Sadly, in Western culture we have essentially amputated our corporate prayer leg and are often lame on our private prayer leg. A healthy and biblical balance in prayer requires diligence in both.

Theologian D. A. Carson affirmed this principle, "Many facets of Christian discipleship, not the least prayer, are more effectively passed on by modeling than from teaching. Good praying is more easily caught than taught. We should choose models from whom we can learn."[2]

As Albert Mohler has aptly noted about the model prayer commanded by Jesus,

> There is no first-person singular pronoun in the entire prayer… One of the besetting sins of evangelicalism is our obsession with individualism. This obsession with individualism chronically besets us as evangelicals. The first-person singular pronoun reigns in our thinking. We tend to think about nearly everything (including the truths of God's Word) only as they relate to me. This is why when Jesus teaches his disciples to pray, He emphasizes from the very outset that we are part of a corporate people called the church.[3]

We learn best to pray by breaking the chains of rugged individualism and consistently gathering with others to learn to pray, to grow more effective in prayer, and to enjoy the richness of a fellowship only experienced together in prayer – especially Scripture-fed, Spirit-led, worship-based prayer.

While we know this experience of praying the Psalms will enrich your personal prayer life, we also encourage you to join others on a very regular basis to practice this biblical approach to prayer. Of course, we trust this tool will be helpful in your marriage, family, and close friendships. If you do not already participate in a group at your church – start one, utilizing this resource. In this way, you can play an essential role in helping your faith community become "a house of prayer for all nations."

---

2. D. A. Carson, *A Call to Spiritual Reformation* (Grand Rapids: Baker, 1992), 35.

3. Mohler, "The Danger of 'I' in Christian Prayer," Albert Mohler https://albertmohler. com/2018/08/20/danger-christian-prayer/ August 20, 2018.

CONTRIBUTORS

Daniel Henderson
GENERAL EDITOR
President, **Strategic Renewal,** *Global Director,* **The 6:4 Fellowship**
(www.strategicrenewal.com) (www.64fellowship.com)

Justin Jeppesen—Director of Spiritual Formation and Adjunct Professor, University of Northwestern, St. Paul, MN (www.unwsp.edu)
Introduction, Appendices A and B, Psalms 42, 55, 59, 67

Dennis Henderson—National Director The 6:4 Fellowship and Leader Development Northlake Church Lago Vista, TX (www.mynorthlake.com)
Psalms 44, 45, 47, 48

Jon Hoekema—Pastor, Horizon Community Church, Downers Grove, IL (www.Horizoncc.org)
Psalms 70, 71, 72

Mike Mitchener—Pastor, Riverview Baptist Church, Ripplemead, VA (www.riverviewtoday.org)
Psalms 53, 54, 58, 65

Mike Moran—Pastor, Creekside Evangelical Free Church, Merced, CA (www.creeksidemerced.org)
Psalms 52, 56, 57, 61

Jeremiah Porter—Pastor, Christ's Community Church, Granite Falls, WA (www.cfccchurch.org)
Psalms 46, 51, 63

Sandy Robertson—Pastor, New Covenant Fellowship, Titusville, FL (www.ncftitusville.org)
Psalms 49, 68, 69

S. Lindsay Taylor—President, Strategic Renewal, Canada, (www. strategicrenewal.ca)
Psalms 43, 50, 66

Aaron Telecky—Pastor, Maranatha Bible Church, Cedar Rapids, IA (www.maranathabible.org)
Psalms 60, 62, 64

INTRODUCTION
By Justin Jeppesen

Music is one of the most powerful mediums of communication. It resonates in our core, eliciting emotion and longing. It calls forth transcendent thoughts and sometimes it even generates movement that alters the trajectory of our lives. Also, music draws out memories.

Have you ever heard a song on the radio or on a playlist that suddenly brings to the surface a memory that you had forgotten? Songs are often attached to memories, and memories bring alive past experiences, both the bad and the good. Imagine if you could go back through your life and write a song for each defining moment – every heartache, every celebration, trial, battle, victory. God already has. *For you.* It's called the Book of Psalms.

Music was a vital component of ancient Hebrew worship. In fact, the Book of Psalms could rightly be considered the original Old Testament "hymnal." Chapters were written in poetic form and most often sung as a part of Israel's worship and celebration. And, like much music written through the centuries, it is no wonder that God, the divine musician, has wonderfully woven themes of joy and remembrance into His songs too.

Each psalm "song" evokes memories of God's gracious dealings with His people, the nation of Israel. All collectively tell how God worked for His glory and their good throughout the multitude of their generations. Today, it could be said, Psalms is the "soundtrack" of God's redemptive history.

Just as songs, when we hear them, draw us back to reflect again on significant events in our personal lives, so too God sang songs over His nation calling them to remember Him and His ways. Yet these songs or Psalms were not only written *to* ancient Israel, they were also divinely composed *for* us. God has arranged divinely inspired songs for every season of our lives. Each psalm has a unique way of giving breath and language to our life of prayer with our Creator. In the same way song lyrics or melodies enable us to articulate the deepest emotions of our hearts or clarify or even simplify puzzling concepts, so too the Psalms engage us at deep levels, especially when drawing us into the broad vocal register of prayer.

It would not be an overstatement to say that Psalms is one of the most popular and beloved books of the Bible. It is the "go to" book for many seeking encouragement and renewal of perspective. It draws from a wealth of experiences that apply to every aspect of human life. But the Psalms are not laid out in a neat and tidy order. Rather they appear unpredictable and dynamic as they flow from one theme to the next. This sense of random order seems to be strangely intentional. Individual Psalms often depict the reality and the dynamic unpredictability of life. Just as life may flow from a joyous occasion one moment, then – even suddenly – into a sorrowful moment the next, the Psalms meet us with a sincere and honest relevancy no matter our circumstances. In reading and thinking about the Psalms, many have found refuge and strength, encouragement in tough times, and especially, abiding joy.

This reality includes you! Even now, as you read this introduction, the Lord is inviting you to encounter Him as you prayerfully engage in His divine songbook. The God of the Psalms desires to sing over you wherever you are in your journey and to bring you into a place of deeper trust and intimacy with Him.

THE PATHWAY TO JOYFUL PRAYER

While the 150 songs that compose the Book of Psalms display a striking diversity of themes, they also present a unified focus. The original Hebrew title for Psalms is "*Tehillim,*" which translates into "Songs of Joy," or even more concisely, "Praises."[1] This is true even though the Psalms of lament, expressing sorrow, outnumber Psalms of praise, accompanied by celebrations of joy. And their order, sequence, and emphasis present a curious, yet insightful surprise. More times lament is the theme of early Psalms (there are 16 in the first 41 chapters). But only 4 are found in the final 43 chapters. Inversely, Psalms of joy are few at the beginning (only 7 in the first 41 chapters). Yet 13 erupt near the end of the entire collection, traveling an increasing crescendo of praise.

The point is this: lament, sorrow, and difficulty are eventually eclipsed by praise, joy, and gratitude at the end. One cannot help but wonder if this order intentionally models our life of faith as traveling pilgrims in this foreign land journeying toward our heavenly home. It is clear that songs of lament and praise go hand in hand to sustain a Godward focus in our praying.

Even now, human sorrows here on earth forge a trajectory toward a heavenly joy that can invade present circumstances. Learning to pray the Psalms as God's *Songs of Joy* equips His people to lay hold of the stunning truths, strengths, and the multitude of comforts He designed to be tangibly experienced in everyday lives.

---

1. Tremper Longman III and Raymond B. Dillard, *An Introduction to the Old Testament* (Grand Rapids, MI: Zondervan, 2006), 238.

PRAYING LIKE JESUS

O f all the Scriptures cited in the New Testament, Psalms tops the list. The Lord Jesus himself quotes this joy-filled book over 50 times, often during occasions of great personal turmoil. They were, for Him, the songs of God, reminding Him of His Father and of Home. As a poignant example, Jesus quotes from the Psalms at the time of His greatest suffering on the cross. And what empowered Jesus to endure the agony of Calvary? According to Hebrews 12:2, it was "the joy that was set before him." Jesus was "a man of sorrows and acquainted with grief" (Isaiah 53:3), and yet, we powerfully see lament and joy converge at the cross. No wonder Jesus uses the Psalms in His dying breaths to extol His firm reliance upon and ultimate trust in His heavenly Father (Psalm 22:1; Psalm 31:5). Even for Jesus the Psalms gave voice to His conversations with His Father and the Scriptures have been recorded to give us His example to emulate.

It's been said that if we can learn to pray as Jesus prayed we will have the power to live as Jesus lived. The good news is that Jesus did not leave His disciples guessing when it came to understanding *how* He prayed. He gave them the very rhythm of prayer modeled by His life and His words, especially found in what is commonly referred to as "The Lord's Prayer" (Matthew 6:9-13 – also Luke 11:2-4). The kind of prayer that Jesus' life exemplified was Scripture-fed, Spirit-led, and worship-based. To the degree that we pray Scripture will be to the degree that we pray like Jesus. While more about Jesus' rhythm of prayer that He commanded us to follow is expounded upon in the next section (see How to Use This Guide), suffice it to say that the Psalms provide an invaluable entry point to begin praying the way Jesus prayed.

A PERSONAL STORY OF TRANSFORMATION

I t was the book of Psalms that the Holy Spirit used to teach me how to pray like Jesus prayed by engaging the Scriptures. When I was first introduced to Strategic Renewal and The 6:4 Fellowship, my life of prayer was transformed as I re-learned how to pray after Jesus' own pattern. The first place I applied this new way of praying was with the Psalms. As I began to practice worship-based prayer in God's songbook, it opened before me a whole new realm of conversation with my Creator. It was like I was beginning to participate in the conversation that God had already initiated with me. Rather than coming to the Lord with a list of needs or feeling puzzled about what I should say, I began coming to Him with fresh eyes of faith, beholding His beauty, and with eager ears to listen to His voice. It was as if the Holy Spirit, as the divine conductor, began leading me through the sheet music of the Psalms to pray according to the diverse, yet unified melody of joy. When I allowed the Spirit-inspired words in the Psalms to shape the way I prayed, I began conversing with Jesus like He may have with His heavenly Father.

Praying the Psalms has cultivated, for me, a deep intimacy with God, established authentic connection with others, and has further equipped me for fruitful service within the local church. No matter what circumstance I have been in the Lord has met me time and again by animating my soul with songs of lament *and* joyful praise.

I referenced earlier the inverse, yet complementary relationship that is found between songs of lament and songs of praise. In 2020 I experienced this dynamic in a powerful and deeply personal way. After battling cancer for several months, the Lord brought my grandmother to her heavenly home. During my final conversation with her I read Psalms 145 through 150. As I read, I often felt compelled to pause, praying a particular passage over her again. As I neared the end I was profoundly struck with the repetition of a single phrase, "Praise the Lord!" In those last moments with my grandmother, lament and sadness were overcome with a supernatural joy and peace. I realized that her faint and final breaths were, nonetheless, exclamations of the strongest praise as she was preparing to meet her Savior face-to-face. The final moments of my grandma's life on earth were matching the crescendo of praise we find in Psalms 145-150.

Just days later I awoke early in the morning to find a message on my phone saying that she had departed for heaven. My knees hit the floor. The first words that passed through my lips were, I believe, the same words my grandmother was then saying at that very moment, "Praise the Lord!" The Lord used the Psalms not only to shape the last conversation I had with her, but also to further fuel a lasting joy and praise that sustains my soul.

BEGINNING YOUR JOURNEY

Taking the cue from the original purpose of Psalms as a book of promise and joyful remembrance for ancient Israel, it has been my desire in recent years to regularly read and pray through the Psalms for the rest of my life. It is my prayer that this guide, and those that follow, combined with the recording of your own personal prayer journey in the "Journal for Experiencing Scripture-fed, Spirit-led, Worship-based Prayer," will mobilize you and other members of the Body of Christ to engage in transforming conversations with God that will have lifelong and multi-generational impact.

HOW TO USE THIS PRAYER GUIDE

Prayer begins in Scripture. For it is in the Bible that our Lord shows His disciples how to pray. In Matthew 6:9-13 – often known as "the Lord's Prayer" – Jesus provides a pattern for prayer and commands that His disciples "pray in this way" (v. 9).

There are four "movements" that compose this divine symphony modeled in Christ's prayer. *Reverence. Response. Requests. Readiness.* Praying through each of these sequentially follows the pattern Christ Himself established. In obedience, when we pray in this way, we are praying God's way. Note the intent of each of the four movements:

"Our Father in heaven, hallowed be your name."
<u>Reverence</u> (Upward) begins with acknowledging the wonder, majesty, and character of God. With an open Bible in front of us, we ask: "Who are you Lord God? What have you revealed about Yourself in this section of Scripture? How do I honor You?"

"Your kingdom come, Your will be done on earth as it is in heaven." <u>Response</u>

(Downward) arises from the worshiping human heart. All I am surrendering to the revelation of all He is. In this movement we yield our will to His, our mind and agenda to Him. Often this response can be guided by the passage in front of us and by asking, "Given what these verses say about You, how do You want me to respond to You today, Father?"

"Give us this day our daily bread and forgive us our debts as we also have forgiven our debtors." *Requests* (Inward) emerge as the simple answers to the question, "What should I pray about?" Allow the verses you are considering in the moment to guide your *requests* in connection to both resources and relationships.

"And lead us not into temptation, but deliver us from evil (or 'the evil one')." This is a cry for *Readiness*, (Outward) to be made ready for spiritual battle. What will we face today in a sinful and hostile world? Strong encouragement can be gleaned from the text we have been considering in this moment of prayer. That is why "praying the Scriptures" is so vital, and why Jesus commanded we follow this pattern. It is God's way to best overcome the attacks of the enemy. And in this way we are energized all the more when reading – or memorizing even – God's Word (Matthew 4:1-10; Ephesians 6:17).

When we "pray in this way," we are following Jesus' clear pattern for His disciples. That is why "the Lord's Prayer" remains a model and pattern for all future prayer, pray-ers, and praying.

Did those disciples in the early chapters of Matthew understand what Jesus was getting at with this prayer pattern? Did they employ this model in their subsequent prayers? It seems so. Found in Acts 4:24-31 is the first recorded prayer of the disciples. It occurs upon the release of Peter and John from trial and confinement by the religious leaders of their day. This is how they prayed:

> And when they heard it, they lifted their voices together to God and said, "Sovereign Lord, who made the heaven and the earth and the sea and everything in them,

– REVERENCE

> who through the mouth of our father David, your servant, said by the Holy Spirit, 'Why did the Gentiles rage, and the peoples plot in vain? The kings of the earth set themselves, and the rulers were gathered together, against the Lord and against his Anointed'— for truly in this city there were gathered together against your holy servant Jesus, whom

you anointed, both Herod and Pontius Pilate, along with the Gentiles and the peoples of Israel, to do whatever your hand and your plan had predestined to take place.

– RESPONSE

And now, Lord, look upon their threats and grant to your servants to continue to speak your word with all boldness while you stretch out your hand to heal, and signs and wonders are performed through the name of your holy servant Jesus."

– REQUESTS

And when they had prayed, the place in which they were gathered together was shaken, and they were all filled with the Holy Spirit and continued to speak the word of God with boldness.

– READINESS

In **Praying the Psalms** we invite you to experience *Scripture-Fed, Spirit-Led, Worship-based Prayer.* It is designed to guide you through each of the four model prayer movements, using the individual Psalms to provoke your prayers.

The psalms are individually set apart for you to encounter God personally and speak with Him. Supplemental commentary by 6:4 Fellowship pastors is provided for additional insight. The variety of approaches and interactions with each Psalm reflects the variety of gifts, viewpoints, and experiences of the contributors, which itself mirrors the multi-faceted Body of Christ. You may choose to meditate on and pray through a single psalm for several days using the multiple prayer prompts provided.

There are two pages set aside for you to interact with each psalm – a "left-hand page" and a "right-hand page." The following is a suggested method for **Praying the Psalms**. We invite you to "pray in this way."

- Select a psalm you wish to pray through (in any order you may choose). Read it from your preferred translation or version of the Bible. (Perhaps read it more than once.)

- Read the brief comments section found on the "left-hand page." There is room in the margins of that page for any personal notes you might wish to record.

- On the "right-hand page," under the <u>*Reverence*</u> (Upward) heading you will see several thoughts about God that are in that particular psalm, His character, His attributes, His Holy Person. Ponder those. Celebrate Him.

- Next, you will see various suggestions ("prompts") for how you might declare back to the Lord the characteristics this particular psalm has revealed about Him. Pick one or two and rejoice in Him, for He is worthy of our praise.

- Similarly, as you move down that page and come to the <u>*Response*</u> (Downward) section, there are several prompts that may stimulate your soul's reflection. Pick one or two and thank God for who He is and how He has delighted your heart.

- As you arrive at the <u>*Requests*</u> (Inward) portion of your prayer time, remember He already knows your needs. (He knows how many hairs you have on your head! – Matthew 10:30, Luke 12:7). Here, use one or two of the suggested prompts to align your heart with His purposes, asking Him for His help and His outcomes in your life.

- <u>*Readiness*</u>, (Outward) is the final movement of prayer. Spiritual war is real, and prayer is our most effective weapon against the diversions, distractions, and divisions of the adversary (2 Corinthians 10:3-5, Ephesians 6:18). Pray through one or two of the prompts inviting God's mercy and protection for yourself and His empowering for resistance against the enemy in the battle for our lives.

We trust you will enjoy and appreciate ***Praying the Psalms*** as you encounter our wonderful Lord. It is our prayer that you flourish in a lifetime of praying God's way, following the example of Jesus, serving others in and by the Holy Spirit, and glorifying the Father (Matthew 5:14-16). Blessings to you in the journey and in the delight of prayer that awaits you.

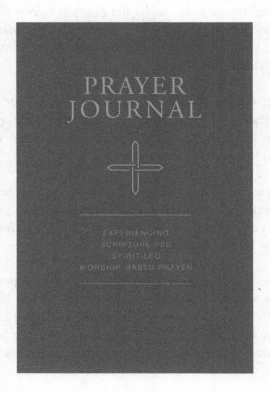

A separate and companion book,
Prayer Journal for Experiencing Scripture-Fed,
Spirit-Led, Worship-Based Prayer,
is also available. We encourage its use in
recording your ongoing encounters with God,
both as you are in the midst of prayer and as you reflect back on how
He has made Himself known to you and answered your prayers.

(store.strategicrenewal.com)

To record your personal reflections as you are
Praying the Psalms, sample pages of this
Prayer Journal are available beginning on page 98

PSALM 42

Author   Sons of Korah

Category   Lament

Summary A song of deep and hopeful longing for God even when the Lord seems distant and our souls feel parched

Have you ever felt distant from God and like you've had a drought at the soul level? This song of lament opens the second book of the Psalms with evocative imagery of a soul's longing to be close to God again. The opening lines paint a picture in our mind's eye for one who craves communion with God yet is inwardly grieved by an apparent lack of access to the Creator.

The language of "pant" and "thirst" conveys not only the author's craving for intimacy with God but also the painstaking reality of his parched soul. As one of the sons of Korah, this author would have likely been among the temple gatekeepers and worship leaders (1 Chron. 25: 1; 26:1). In contrast to his longing to come before God again, tears of grief became his "food." Instead of leading among the chorus of temple praise, voices of taunting filled his ears.

In response to the turmoil of his oppressors, the psalmist chose to remember (vv. 4, 6) sweet and satisfying times of communion with God. Remembering not only seems to have heightened the psalmist's agony but also called forth the twice repeated chorus of resurrecting hope (vv. 5, 11). Instead of turning merely inward and giving way to the decay of inner voices of deceit, this son of Korah used his voice to proclaim truth over his soul, inciting a confident trust in the Lord. Even though he was enduring the incessant taunting of his enemies over the apparent distance of God's presence (vv. 3, 10), and perhaps feeling the merciful weight of God's discipline (v. 7), the reality of Lord's steadfast love occupied his mind day and night (v. 8).

Psalm 42 is often thought to be directly linked to Psalm 43, and, sometimes, these are thought of as a single psalm. The same chorus of hope is repeated in Psalm 43 (v. 5), sharing an identical ending with Psalm 42. Praying the words of this Psalm can secure the pathway for our parched souls to be satisfied in God alone. So, no matter what state your soul is in, may you allow this honest chorus of resurrecting hope to have the final word.

PSALM 42 – GUIDE

REVERENCE – *Identify and celebrate God's praiseworthy attributes*

- Satisfier of our souls – v. 1
- Living God, present and approachable – v. 2
- Worthy of glad shouts and songs of praise – v. 3
- Our hope, our salvation – vv. 6, 11
- Provider of steadfast love – v. 8
- Our life and our rock – vv. 8–9
- Sovereign over suffering – vv. 3, 9–10

Prayer Prompts
- Lord, my soul longs for You because You are …
- Lord, thank You for satisfying my soul when …
- Lord, thank You for fulfilling my hope for …
- Because You are the God of hope, I will praise You even when …
- Lord, thank You for saving me from …
- God of my life, thank You for being with me in my suffering of …

RESPONSE – *Surrender to Him and His ways*

- Lord, I admit my soul is cast down about … and ask that You help me to hope in You!
- Lord, when others ask, "Where is your God?" I will remember that You …
- I confess that I felt forgotten by You when … and say again that You are my rock!

REQUESTS – *Ask the Spirit to guide your prayer over concerns, resources, and relationships*

- Satisfy my soul's longing for …
- Lord, bring Your hope and salvation to …
- As I pour out my soul to You about … remind me that I am not alone!
- Lord, command Your steadfast love to me as I face the suffering of …
- Help me see Your face today as I struggle with …
- Lord, be my rock today when I feel overwhelmed about …
- In my pain and distress, help me to hope in You for …

READINESS – *Encouragement and strength for spiritual battle*

- Lord, I trust You today to be my hope, especially when …
- Lord, help me remember Your steadfastness today as I face the adversary of …
- When my soul is cast down about … help me trust in Your salvation!

PSALM 43

Author   Unknown, possibly David
Category   Wisdom/Lament
Summary   Remarkably similar to Psalm 42; a sadly beautiful poem in which the writer has been exiled and longs to return to Jerusalem

This psalm is terribly similar to its predecessor and may be a continuation. David, who probably was the author, was being chased and driven out of his country by the unjust violence and tyranny of his enemies. He called upon God for vengeance and encouraged himself to hope for restoration.

When reading psalms such as this, we can see the danger in telling God's people that they will be happy all the time. Yes, they have the abundant life, but they are not always "happy." Yes, God is always with us; but that doesn't mean we always feel that presence! It's much easier to feel like a Christian when everything is going great in our lives. However, our faith is tested and grows during the difficult times when God seems far off. We must trust good theology and know that He is with us and abiding in us, even when we don't feel Him.

This psalmist reminded himself to hope in God and praise Him alone. That is a picture of true faith in the Lord. Even when the days are dark and grim, praise God who alone is your help and strength.

Pray today that your heart and soul will be lifted up in praise to God no matter what the day brings to you.

PSALM 43 – GUIDE

REVERENCE – *Identify and celebrate God's praiseworthy attributes*

- He is God and Deliverer – v. 1
- Our strength, holy, and the giver of light and truth – vv. 2–3
- The joy giver and worthy of praise – v. 4
- The God of hope and our helper – v. 5

Prayer Prompts

- I will praise You, Father, because You are my stronghold when ...
- I praise You that You are the God of ...
- Thank You for sending Your light into my life when I was ...
- I worship You as the God of hope because You have guided me through ...

RESPONSE – *Surrender to Him and His ways*

- I come to Your altar and confess ...
- I confess I am disturbed by my ... help me Lord!
- I often turn to ... before I look to You for guidance.
- When I encounter ... my joy and delight are impacted. Forgive me.

REQUESTS – *Ask the Spirit to guide your prayer over concerns, resources, and relationships*

- Since You are my stronghold, please help me run to You when ...
- God, I ask that Your light and truth will guide me as I navigate the waters of ...
- Father, in the moments when my circumstances fill me with ... turn my eyes to You and give me hope.
- I pray You will give light to (name) so that they will turn to You.
- As the God of hope I bring ... to You and ask Your will to be done.

READINESS – *Encouragement and strength for spiritual battle*

- Give me joy, O Lord, as I serve You today in ... even when ...
- Remind me throughout this day that Your light and truth are greater than ...

PSALM 44

Author   Unknown

Category   Lament

Summary   A remembrance of what God has done in the past, a statement of confidence in God the great King, a lament, a protest, and a cry for help in the present situation

This psalm begins as a national remembrance of God's intervention for His people when He delivered them from Egypt and drove their enemies out of the land. In these positive memories, the authors acknowledged it was God's strong right hand and arm that worked on their behalf. The remembrance is fitting and reveals that their forefathers were faithful in telling the next generation about God's work for them. This is a good reminder for us to do the same in teaching and praying for the coming generation.

In this community lament, it is noticeable that the speaker in verses 4 and 6 is singular. It could be that David, Israel's king, broke in and addressed the King of glory. As the king of the nation, it was appropriate for him to lead the people in asking for God's renewed favor. The king affirmed that his confidence was not in his sword or bow. Clearly, in verse 7, the psalmist(s) recognized that it was God who saved them from their enemies.

The basis of this lament begins in verse 9 and continues to verse 22. God's people were being defeated in battle and scattered among the nations. They felt like they were cast off and sold out by God. They were being made a reproach among the nations. They protested because they felt they had not forgotten God or turned their hearts away from Him. They questioned why all of the wrong had come to them.

There will be times in our lives when "bad" things come upon us while we are trying to serve God to the fullest. We are seeking His will for our lives, and it seems like one thing after another goes wrong from finances to family challenges to sickness. Our minds are spinning, our hearts are becoming weary, and questions are growing. There are no quick answers nor magic formulas. Turn your attention to the first part of the psalm. Remember what God has done for you in the past. Dwell at verse 8 and begin to praise and boast of your great God. Know that He is able to turn any situation around in a moment. Trust the goodness of God and call on Him as Israel did in verses 23–26.

We trust based on remembrance of His past deeds and obey because doing so always develops the character we need to endure. Finally, we wait, and God puts us on display as people who believe there is much more than we see. We cast our eyes on the unseen, which is eternal. What we are seeing, feeling, and bearing is temporal.

PSALM 44 – GUIDE

REVERENCE – *Identify and celebrate God's praiseworthy attributes*

- God from ancient times, performing mighty deeds for His children – vv. 1–3
- King, Savior, Victor, worthy of trust and thanksgiving – vv. 4–8
- Discipliner of those He loves – vv. 9–20
- Knows the secrets of the human heart – v. 21
- Helps and redeems in His steadfast love – v. 26

Prayer Prompts

- Praise, Lord, for Your mighty deeds on behalf of Your people, especially ...
- I praise You because You are King over ...
- Because Your name is ... You are able to overcome the enemy of ...
- Lord, we boast in You because ...

RESPONSE – *Surrender to Him and His ways*

- Father, I confess that too often I trust in my bow (v. 6), especially when I rely on ...
- You know the secrets of my heart; I admit today I am struggling with questions about ...

REQUESTS – *Ask the Spirit to guide your prayer over concerns, resources, and relationships*

- Because of Your strong right hand and the light of Your face, I am trusting You today to save me from ...
- Lord, remind me that You delight in me, especially when I am feeling ...
- I pray that (name) will trust in Your name so that they will overcome the enemy of ...
- Lord, we ask You to "rise up" (v. 26) and help our ministry as we ...

READINESS – *Encouragement and strength for spiritual battle*

- Father, when I don't understand and have doubts about ... I will trust You to rise up and help me overcome ...
- For the sake of Your steadfast love, redeem us when we face ...

PSALM 45

Author   Sons of Korah
Category   Royal
Summary   A wedding psalm for David; one of the messianic psalms presenting Jesus as the bridegroom and the church as His bride

In stark contrast with the previous psalm of lament, this psalm is full of celebration. As the psalm opens, we see words addressed to the King. After this, the psalmist went on to describe attributes of the King in verses 2–9. Compare verses 6–7 to Hebrews 1:8–9:

> But of the Son he says, Your throne, O God, is forever and ever, the scepter of uprightness is the scepter of your kingdom.
>
> You have loved righteousness and hated wickedness; therefore God, your God, has anointed you with the oil of gladness beyond your companions."

Reading through this psalm should grow an awareness of praise in our hearts and on our lips. Tell God how good He is and how much we adore Him. He does not need our praise. But we need to praise Him as it develops a heart of gratitude and humility. Our acknowledging His greatness first gives us the confidence to bring Him our requests as the all-wise God.

In verses 10–15, the song turns our attention to the bride ("O daughter"). Her loyalty is now to her bridegroom and no longer to her father. She is joined to a new authority. This is a clear picture of Christ and His church. As Christ followers, His bride, we should bring forth great words of praise to the One who will present us faultless before the throne of God.

As the psalm closes, the song turns back once again to the king David. Verses 16–17 express the continuation of the line of David, which holds with it significant messianic expectations. The nation of Israel had hope through the lineage of David; we now have hope in Christ our King! Note the great conclusion in verse 17: "I will cause Your name to be remembered in all generations; therefore nations will praise you forever and ever."

This should be the outcome of our worship and prayer. This should be for what we pray.

PSALM 45 – GUIDE

REVERENCE – *Identify and celebrate God's praiseworthy attributes*

- God fills our hearts with pleasantries and is a King to whom we can turn – v. 1
- He pours out His grace and blessings – v. 2
- He is a God of truth, humility, justice, and awesome deeds – v. 4
- Eternal, upright, and righteous – vv. 6–7
- God anoints us with the oil of gladness, value, and beauty – vv. 7, 15
- He gives us royal identities and significance – vv. 16–17

Prayer Prompts

- We are a blessed people because Your name is …
- We praise You because You are our … (e.g., King, etc.).
- I lift up Your name, Lord, because You poured out Your grace on me even when I …

RESPONSE – *Surrender to Him and His ways*

- I confess the sin of … (form of unrighteous) that stands in opposition to the things You love.
- I confess that I did not recognize my royal value when I fell prey/condemned to/in …

REQUESTS – *Ask the Spirit to guide your prayer over concerns, resources, and relationships*

- Help me to walk in truth, humility, and justice today as I …
- Because You lift up Your people, would You lift up …
  as they endure …
- Fill me with joy today as I walk through …
- Would You help (name) see their value and beauty in Your eyes as they struggle with …

READINESS – *Encouragement and strength for spiritual battle*

- Lord, I am trusting that You will overflow me with Your grace today so that I can pour out Your grace on …
- Lord, fill my heart with the knowledge that I'm blessed by You, especially as I walk through …

PSALM 46

Author   The Sons of Korah
Category   Confidence
Summary   Finding confidence in God when life is overwhelmingly stressful

Stress is a killer – literally! Chronic stress is the root cause of more than 60 percent of all illness and disease.[2] Life's stresses are experienced in a variety of forms, such as the loss of a job, death of a loved one, financial problems, moving to a new location, chronic illness or pain, mental or emotional struggles, and traumatic events. In the midst of overwhelming stress, we need to remember the words of Psalm 46.

The psalm begins by remembering God as our "refuge and strength" and as the One who is always present and available to help. It is because God is God that the psalmist boldly declared that even in the most turbulent, disruptive, and life-shaking experiences, we need not fear. It is God's presence and power that provides assurance and confidence for His people in seasons of utter distress.

Our natural instinct when overwhelmingly stressed is usually one of two responses – fight or flight. But in verse 10 God spoke a very clear command, "Be still, and know that I am God." Instead of rushing into a frenzy of panic and fear, we are to literally stop everything and direct our hearts and minds to remember that God is God. We are commanded to stand still in peace by remembering that God is everything He has revealed Himself to be. If we want to dwell in peace and confidence even as life gets crazy, we must remember and choose to trust that God will always be God and that He will always be with us and will help us.

---

2 HeartMath LLC, "How Stress Affects the Body," HuffPost, last updated December 6, 2017, https://www.huffpost.com/entry/how-stress-affects-the-body_b_2422522.

PSALM 46 – GUIDE

REVERENCE – *Identify and celebrate God's praiseworthy attributes*

- Our refuge and strength – v. 1
- An ever-present help and security – vv. 1, 5, 7, 11
- A God of gladness and holiness – v. 4
- An almighty fortress – vv. 7, 11
- Mighty in His works – vv. 8–9
- Forever sovereign and exalted – v. 10

  Prayer Prompts
- God, thank You for being with me and being my refuge when ...
- Because You are my very present help, I praise You that I do not have to be afraid of ...
- I praise You today for Your mighty works in my life, especially ...
- Lord Almighty, I exalt You today because You are sovereign over ...

RESPONSE – *Surrender to Him and His ways*

- I confess that I am often afraid of ... Fix my eyes on You.
- Lord, even though ... I will trust that You are in control.

REQUESTS – *Ask the Spirit to guide your prayer over concerns, resources, and relationships*

- God, right now I need to rest in the truth of Your indwelling presence as I ...
- Lord, let (name) experience You as their refuge and strength as ...
- Help me be still and stop my striving, trusting Your sovereign plan, especially as I struggle with ...
- Lord, today the nation of ... is on my heart. I pray that You will be exalted as the power of the gospel goes forth.

READINESS – *Encouragement and strength for spiritual battle*

- Lord, because of Your indwelling presence, I know You are my fortress and I will not be shaken even when I encounter ...
- Because of Your mighty works in the past, I will trust You to work again even when the enemy tries to ...

PSALM 47

Author   Sons of Korah
Category Praise
Summary   God is King over all the earth and all humanity is called to praise Him

This beautiful psalm celebrates a great victory. Reflecting on a triumph of a king such as David, the psalmist prophetically has in mind the ascension of the Messiah to His throne and celebrates His reign over the whole earth.

All the earth is called to worship (vv. 1–3, 7–9). Those who are to worship are those who are saved. This is our core purpose as Christians. Eventually the whole earth, saved and unsaved, will call Him Lord, according to Philippians 2:9. Similarly, in Revelation, John saw people from every tribe, nation, and tongue worshipping the King (7:9). This is truly the heart of God. He so loved the world that He is not willing for any should perish. Again, our worship should take us to His heart, and we should live and pray with this in mind.

Worship has many expressions; clapping hands (v. 1); shouting to God (v. 1); singing praises (vv. 6–7); using our minds (v. 7). Jesus instructed us to love the Lord our God with all our heart, all our soul, all our mind, and all our strength (Luke 10:27). Worship can never be half-hearted. Worship is the expression of all I am in response to all He is.

Surely worship needs new attitudes. The psalmist mentioned two: joy (v. 1) and fear (v. 2). Joy is an internal mind that joins with peace and is seeking God's will rather than our own. God is central in our worship and desires. We should seek to honor Him and Him alone. This will bring a sense satisfaction. Fear is the basis of awe, reverence, and respect that results in bended knees and humbled hearts.

The psalmist was confident in the wisdom and goodness of the great King. He was happy to let the great King choose the inheritance of His people, as described in Ephesians 1:3–6:

- He chose us in Him before the foundation of the world.
- He chose us to be holy and blameless before Him in love.
- He chose us to be adopted as sons into His family.

The last sentence in this psalm is a banner that should fly over us: "He is highly exalted." Today, as you pray, read this psalm a few times. Let God's promise of His inheritance reserved in heaven for you sink into your heart.

PSALM 47 – GUIDE

REVERENCE – *Identify and celebrate God's praiseworthy attributes*

- He is worthy of praise, reverential awe, and worship – vv. 1–2, 6–7
- Our source of joy – v. 1
- Sovereign, the Most High, King, Ruler, and holy – vv. 2, 7–8
- He fights our battles, saves, and loves us – vv. 3–4
- He is faithful to His covenant and highly exalted – v. 9

Prayer Prompts

- God, I shout to You with joy today because …
- Lord, I give You reverence and awe because You are …
- I will praise You because You are the great King over …
- Because You love us, we have seen You are working in …

RESPONSE – *Surrender to Him and His ways*

- Because You are the King of kings, it is right that I surrender … to You today.
- I confess my inclination to exalt myself, instead of You, when I …

REQUESTS – *Ask the Spirit to guide your prayer over concerns, resources, and relationships*

- Lord, give me new grace to sing and shout for joy even when …
- Because You fight our battles, I pray that You will deliver (name) from …
- Give me a heart to fear You this week as I …

READINESS – *Encouragement and strength for spiritual battle*

- Remind me today that You chose me and love me when the enemy seeks to …
- Because You reign in holiness, I will trust in You to rule my heart and mind when I am tempted with …

PSALM 48

Author   Sons of Korah
Category   Praise
Summary   A celebration of God's greatness in the holy city of Jerusalem, which is the city of God

Psalm 48 begins with the praise of God and His greatness (v. 1) and ends with the praise of God and His goodness as our great Guide forever (v. 14). The city of Jerusalem has always been remarkable. The psalm connects it with the praises to God due to the care and protection the city enjoys from God. This is the city of the Great King. When kings of the earth assembled and saw the city, they were astonished. They panicked and fled (vv. 4–5).

In our day of injustice, social unrest, and division, we should rejoice that a day is coming when God will bring justice to the world. What a great joy it will be for God's people when Jesus reigns in His rightful place (v. 11; Rev. 21:1–3).

We pray often for God's guidance on our situations. What we often mean is we want a map showing all the landmarks on our journey and a companion who knows the way. Here's the good news. The Bible is our map; God, Himself, through His Spirit, is our personal Guide and Companion (v. 14).

As the Temple of the living God, the church will not fail when Jesus builds it (Matt. 16:18). The Roman Empire trembled at the resurrection of Christ. The world witnessed the miracles and the brave martyrdom of the Apostles and trembled. Kings, authorities, and governments tried to stop the spread of the gospel. But nothing could block the extension of Christ's Kingdom. May this truth encourage us as we serve the Lord Jesus in a hostile and dismissive world.

The psalm closes with the proclamation that God is our God forever and ever. No earthly kings can say that their crowns are theirs forever; no landlords can say the land will be theirs forever. Possessions can and do change hands regularly. Indeed, everything that we see will ultimately come to dust (2 Peter 3:10). But God's Kingdom, His reign, will last forever. May we live daily in praise and confidence in our great God!

PSALM 48 – GUIDE

REVERENCE – *Identify and celebrate God's praiseworthy attributes*

- The Lord is great, beautiful, and our joy – vv. 1–2
- Our fortress and defender, the One who establishes His people – vv. 3–8
- A God of steadfast love, righteousness, and judgment – vv. 9–11
- Worthy of praise because of His name – v. 10
- The God of every generation; our Guide now and forever – vv. 13–14

> *Prayer Prompts*

- Great and mighty God, You are to be highly praised because …
- Lord, thank You that You were my fortress and defender when …
- You are worthy of praise because Your name is …
- Thank You for the joy I felt when You …

RESPONSE – *Surrender to Him and His ways*

- Lord, even though You have done so many great works, I sometimes allow … to diminish my joy in You.
- I confess that I sometimes fail to declare Your works to the next generation because …

REQUESTS – *Ask the Spirit to guide your prayer over concerns, resources, and relationships*

- Lord, because You are so great, I will trust You to be my fortress today as I …
- Lord, by Your faithfulness and power, I ask You to establish …
- Because Your name is … I trust Your "right hand" (v. 10) is able to …
- Use me to declare and demonstrate to the next generation that You are …
- I pray that (name) will trust Your guidance today as they …

READINESS – *Encouragement and strength for spiritual battle*

- Lord, let me worship You consistently this day, in assurance of Your steadfast love when the world, the flesh, and the devil try to …
- Because of Your faithful victories in the past, I will trust You to guide me, especially as I struggle with …

PSALM 49

Author Sons of Korah
Category Wisdom
Summary Death is not to be feared for those who put their trust in the Lord; God will receive them into His eternal presence

M y family and I have watched the movie *The Princess Bride* so many times that we could turn the sound off and still quote most of the lines. One line in particular is repeated several times: "Hello, my name is Inigo Montoya, you killed my father, prepare to die!"[3] Good advice from the Spaniard: "prepare to die." We all will (Amos 4:12).

You are prepared to die if you can say with the psalmist, "Why should I be afraid in times of trouble and when I am surrounded by evil?" (v. 5, paraphrased).

You are prepared to die if you can say with the psalmist, "God will redeem my soul from the power of death, for he will receive me." (v. 15 TLB).

You are prepared to die if you can say with the Apostle Paul, "I have the desire to depart and be with Christ, which is better by far" (Phil. 1:23, EHV).

You are prepared to die if you can say with the Apostle Paul, "For me, to live is Christ and to die is gain" (Phil. 1:21 CSB).

You are prepared to die when you understand that "the ransom of a life is too costly, and [the price one can pay] can never suffice—so that he should live on forever and never see the pit (the grave) and corruption" (Ps. 49:8–9 AMPC).

Riches, good works, a good name, cannot buy eternal security. Nothing but the blood of Jesus!

---

3 *The Princess Bride*, directed by Rob Reiner (Los Angeles: 20th Century Fox, 1987), DV, 21:28.

PSALM 49 – GUIDE

REVERENCE – *Identify and celebrate God's praiseworthy attributes*

- Has a message for all, regardless of their position in this world – vv. 1–2
- Gives wisdom and understanding to humanity – v. 3
- His people need not fear in times of trouble – v. 5
- Does not require a ransom paid by us for our own lives – vv. 7–9
- Receives His people in the resurrection – v. 15

Prayer Prompts

- Thank You that even though I may not have … in this world, You still …
- I praise You that You have given me Your wisdom, especially when …
- Lord, I praise You that because of Your truth, I do not have to fear …
- I praise You for Your resurrection power that gives me hope even when …

RESPONSE – *Surrender to Him and His ways*

- Lord, I confess that today I am struggling with some fear about …
- I confess that, like the world, I often look to … instead of trusting in You.

REQUESTS – *Ask the Spirit to guide your prayer over concerns, resources, and relationships*

- Lord, I know that (name) is dealing with fear over … Give them Your wisdom and hope to overcome.
- Lord, today my heart is burdened for (name), who has embraced the values of this world and is facing eternity apart from You. Give me compassion and courage to tell them of Your salvation.
- Lord, as I look around at the fleeting "riches" of the world, give me fresh assurance that …

READINESS – *Encouragement and strength for spiritual battle*

- Deliver me today when I am tempted to have "foolish confidence" (v. 13) in … rather than in Your wisdom.
- Lord, because You have ransomed my soul, give me Your grace to live in victory, especially when I am tempted to …

PSALM 50

Author   Asaph
Category   Prophecy
Summary   A prophetic warning from Asaph about coming judgment for insincere sacrifices and unethical practices with instruction for correction.

P salm 50 is very sobering; one we must take care to act upon. It describes a time to come that we will all experience. God will bring all the souls of men together from heaven above and the earth beneath. No one will escape this courtroom. He is a just God; He will not be bought. The only payment He will receive is from those who have bowed the knee before Christ and cried out to Him for salvation. The Bible tells us that every knee will bow (Phil. 2:10). God then sees the righteousness of Christ when He gazes upon us.

There are only two classes of people in this courtroom: the Godly and the ungodly. He will gather His saints together with Him, but the ungodly will be sent to eternal judgment. This is not a statement designed to scare people; rather, it simply is the truth!

Many today do not believe there is a God because, despite their great sin, they have never been struck by lightning or been judged in any way. God's answer to them when they stand before Him is: "These things you have done, and I kept silent; you thought that I was altogether like you; but I will rebuke you, and set them in order before your eyes" (v. 21 NKJV).

This psalm is ultimately concerned with genuine loyalty.

PSALM 50 – GUIDE

REVERENCE – *Identify and celebrate God's praiseworthy attributes*

- He is the mighty One, beautiful, and glorious – vv. 1–2
- He communicates His will, is a righteous judge, and relates personally – vv. 2–7, 16–22
- Owner of everything, all knowing, and sufficient – vv. 7–13
- Worthy of our gratitude and loyal obedience – vv. 14, 23
- He rescues and judges – v. 15
- The giver of salvation – v. 23

Prayer Prompts

- I praise You that because You are the mighty One, You can …
- You are the perfecting of beauty because …
- I offer my sacrifice of thanksgiving for Your …
- I exalt You today as the …

RESPONSE – *Surrender to Him and His ways*

- I confess that I sometimes go through the motions of worship, but my heart is …
- When I look at Your displeasure with sin in vv. 16–21, I am convicted that I …

REQUESTS – *Ask the Spirit to guide your prayer over concerns, resources, and relationships*

- Lord, I want to please and glorify You today by expressing my gratitude for …
- I pray for (name) who is in a "day of trouble" (v. 15), asking that you will … for Your glory.
- I know You want me to order my way rightly, to give me grace to …

READINESS – *Encouragement and strength for spiritual battle*

- Today I call on You to deliver me from … that I might glorify You.
- Show me Your saving power as You give me grace to do what is right when I …

PSALM 51

Author David

Category Lament

Summary Seeking God when you have failed miserably

This Psalm was written after David had sinned, committing adultery with Bathsheba and murdering her husband Uriah in attempts to cover up his sin. I know. That is really messed up. In 2 Samuel 12, God brought Nathan to confront David, and eventually David confessed that he had sinned against God. Then in verse 13, Nathan affirmed God's merciful forgiveness for the repentant sinner. Psalm 51 is an account of David's return to the Lord in a prayer of confession and repentance.

The Psalm begins with expressions of deep desperation for God's mercy and forgiveness (vv. 1–7). David appealed to God's "unfailing love" and "great compassion" in his requests (v. 1 NIV). The depth of his anguish can be felt in his recognition that his sin ultimately came down to his rebellion against God (vv. 3–4). David was at the mercy of God. But he understood that God *is* merciful, loving, compassionate and will reconcile to Himself those who truly repent. So, having confessed his sin, David sought the Lord for personal restoration and renewal.

"Spirit" is a key word, used three times in verses 10–12 and once more in verse 17. In asking God to renew in him a "right spirit" (v. 10), David was acknowledging he had been driven by a wrong spirit – one that was not fully surrendered to God. We know from the story in 2 Samuel 11 that David was living in disobedience to God before he ever saw Bathsheba. In verse 11 of this psalm, David acknowledged that his only hope in overcoming sin was the very presence of the Holy Spirit. That said, without a "willing spirit," David knew he would be prone to once again wander from the Holy Spirit right back into sin (v. 12). Finally, in verse 17, David admitted that humility before God was the posture in which he needed to remain – the posture of the heart that pleases God.

PSALM 51 – GUIDE

REVERENCE – *Identify and celebrate God's praiseworthy attributes*

- Merciful, giver of unfailing love and great compassion – v. 1
- He washes/cleanses our sin – vv. 2, 7
- A just judge, a God of truth and wisdom – vv. 4, 6
- A God of joy, gladness, renewal, and restoration – vv. 8–12
- A good God who builds up and delights in His people – vv. 17–18

Prayer Prompts

- God, I praise You for showing me mercy when …
- Thank You, Lord, for cleansing me from …
- I praise You for teaching me the truth about … that has changed me from the inside out.

RESPONSE – *Surrender to Him and His ways*

- Lord, I confess I have sinned against You by …
- Lord, because of Your unfailing love, I'm asking You to forgive me for …
- Lord, I admit that … often threatens the joy of my salvation.

REQUESTS – *Ask the Spirit to guide your prayer over concerns, resources, and relationships*

- Lord, I know I need to deal truthfully in my inmost being about the issue of … so that …
- God, create in me a pure heart that will …
- Because of the mercy I have experienced, open my lips to explain to others that …
- God, restore to (name) the joy of Your salvation!
- Because You are forgiving and good, I know I can trust You to build up …

READINESS – *Encouragement and strength for spiritual battle*

- Save us, O God, from the temptation to …
- In Your good pleasure make us prosper in our battle(s) against …
- God of my salvation, deliver me from … so that I will sing aloud of Your righteousness.

PSALM 52

Author   David

Category   Lament

Summary   After King Saul's servant Doeg revealed David's whereabouts and activity, David wrote a stinging description of Doeg and the future judgment that awaited him; still, David expressed his own confidence and trust in the unfailing love of God to those who remain faithful to Him

"Sticks and stones may break my bones, but words will never hurt me." David, soon to be the king of Israel, would strongly disagree with that old saying above. In Psalm 52, David addressed the actions of Doeg, a servant of King Saul, who by his own words in 1 Samuel 22:9–10, revealed David's activity and whereabouts to Saul. David described Doeg's words in verses 1–4 of this psalm as boasting, evil, plotting destruction, false, harmful, and deceitful. It was Doeg's words that prompted King Saul to go on a murderous rampage against David and all who helped him survive and escape capture. Words prompt actions, and Doeg's words brought about great hurt to many as a result of Saul's response to what Doeg revealed.

In Psalm 52, David then contrasted the outcomes for men like Doeg as against those who make God their stronghold. For Doeg, David wrote that God would "break you down . . . snatch you up and tear you . . . and uproot you" with the end being eternal destruction (v. 5 NASB). The end for those like Doeg would demonstrate the outcome of a life spent trusting in earthly riches and not in the true and lasting riches of their Maker. The end would be different for the faithful, who make God their stronghold. David described their lives as flourishing, trusting, praising and hopeful, a marked difference from Doeg and those who lived and spoke like him.

Words matter, they hurt, they bring about actions that can be destructive. This is why the Scripture is constantly reminding us about the powerful impact of words and their ability to bring about good or evil. Jesus said it succinctly, "Out of the abundance of the heart [the] mouth speaks" (Luke 6:45 NKJV). Let's remember that our words are a true reflection of the condition of our own hearts' motives and desires.

PSALM 52 – GUIDE

REVERENCE – *Identify and celebrate God's praiseworthy attributes*

- A God of steadfast love – vv. 1, 8
- Our defender and our refuge – vv. 5, 7
- One whose love is unfailing – v. 8
- One who has done great things, whose name and goodness are our hope – v. 9

Prayer Prompts

- I praise You for being my stronghold when …
- I praise You for showing me Your unfailing love when …
- My hope is in You because …
- Thank You for defending me from …
- I will thank You forever because You have…

RESPONSE – *Surrender to Him and His ways*

- I admit that sometimes in my day I forget about Your steadfast love, especially when …
- I confess that I often seek refuge and trust in … rather than in You.

REQUESTS – *Ask the Spirit to guide your prayer over concerns, resources, and relationships*

- Because of Your steadfast love I will trust You to defend me from …
- Because my hope is in You, I will not fear …
- God, You are my refuge, so today I will trust You for …
- Today I will wait on the goodness of Your name for …

READINESS – *Encouragement and strength for spiritual battle*

- As the battle rages, grant me protection over the enemy of …
- Today I will trust in Your steadfast love, especially when …

PSALM 53

Author David
Category Historical
Summary This psalm looks forward to the establishment of God's Kingdom

As a young preacher, I described a gentleman to the congregation as "an all-around good guy." Instinctively, Uncle Pat thought *out loud*, "There is none good, no, not one." His words not only penetrated the sanctuary but also sank deep into my heart. Uncle Pat was one of the most righteous men I knew. Every time I visited him, he was at his kitchen table worshiping the Lord, studying his Bible, and writing his own personal commentary on books like Isaiah.

Uncle Pat knew in his flesh he was like everyone else; but, as a believer, he had the privilege to seek the Lord through His Word. So, even though he only had a fourth-grade education, his journal was as deep and insightful as any published theologian's work. Why? Because when God looked down to see if anyone was seeking after Him, He saw Uncle Pat wholeheartedly doing so. And God revealed Himself to this simple, uneducated man.

Even if I think I am an "all-around good guy," I am incapable of entering God's presence in the flesh! God's efforts to find a single person who understands Him or seeks Him in the flesh remain fruitless. However, He does find His children who take the time to seek Him in the Spirit. Let Uncle Pat encourage you to open up your Bible, get out a journal, and start wholeheartedly seeking the Lord today. As you rejoice and be glad, you can practice *Scripture-fed, Spirit-led, Worship-based prayer.*

PSALM 53 – GUIDE

REVERENCE – *Identify and celebrate God's praiseworthy attributes*

- God sees all and seeks those who will seek Him – vv. 1–2
- He judges those who knowingly reject Him – vv. 3–5
- He is the God of salvation to His people – v. 6
- He restores and give us joy and gladness – v. 6

Prayer Prompts

- I praise You that by grace You have called me to seek
- You. Today I seek You because You are …
- You are the God of my salvation and have saved me from …
- I praise You because You have restored …
- Thank You for giving me supernatural joy and gladness, even when …

RESPONSE – *Surrender to Him and His ways*

- I confess that I have been foolish when I have said no to You about …
- I confess that I, too, have failed to understand Your ways when …
- I confess that I try to be good in my own strength when …

REQUESTS – *Ask the Spirit to guide your prayer over concerns, resources, and relationships*

- Today I am seeking You, and I need understanding about …
- I pray for (name), who has rejected Your truth. Use me to show them the joy of Your salvation.
- Lord, today I am trusting You to restore …

READINESS – *Encouragement and strength for spiritual battle*

- Even though I am surrounded by the evils of … give me a passion to seek You.
- I will trust you to give me joy and gladness even when …

PSALM 54

Author David

Category Confidence

Summary As David was pursued by enemies (King Saul) and betrayed by allies (the Ziphites), he remained confident the Lord would deliver him

The "strangers" seeking David's life (v. 3) were actually his kin, the Ziphites, part of David's own tribe of Judah (1 Sam. 23:13–24; 26:1). They told King Saul where David was hiding.

Like David, most of us have been betrayed by close family or friends. It is easy to react to the betrayals with a myriad of emotions: anger, slander, malice, revenge, gossip, fear, worry, anxiety – the list of our emotionally driven, vindictive reactions could go on and on. But the Lord wants us to make a conscious choice to act (not react) like we really believe that at the core of His Name, His essence, His character He is good, faithful, merciful, holy, just, all powerful. The list of His divine attributes can go on and on too. He wants us to *act as if we believe* He is both willing and able to not just save us but vindicate us. David left his enemy in God's hands: "I have not sinned against you, though you hunt my life to take it. May the LORD judge between me and you, may the LORD avenge me against you, but my hand shall not be against you" (1 Sam. 24:11–12).

If we stop and look back, we are reminded of how God has delivered us in the past. If we look forward, we know He will one day deliver us in ultimate triumph over every enemy. So, on the basis of His character, ask God to deliver you and vindicate you in your current circumstances! Instead of being bitter, choose today to freely offer a sacrifice of praise to Him. The Lord is listening to the words of your mouth. So give thanks to His Name for allowing you to go through those hardships, sufferings, and even betrayals so that He can prove His good character *to you* and magnify His mighty name *through you*.

PSALM 54 – GUIDE

REVERENCE – *Identify and celebrate God's praiseworthy attributes*

- God is a savior, mighty, and our vindicator – v. 1
- God hears our prayers and is a faithful helper, upholder, and deliverer – vv. 2–3, 7
- He is good and worthy of our sincere thanks – v. 6

Prayer Prompts
- I praise You that because Your name is … You have saved me from …
- I praise You that You heard my desperate prayers when …
- Thank You for helping and upholding me when I was …

RESPONSE – *Surrender to Him and His ways*

- Rather than trusting in Your vindication, I often try to defend myself when …
- I confess that I do not thank You enough for …

REQUESTS – *Ask the Spirit to guide your prayer over concerns, resources, relationships*

- Today I am feeling under attack over … but will trust You to defend me.
- Lord, because You are my helper, I trust You to …
- Lord, in Your faithfulness, I ask You to uphold (name) as they …
- Today I need a grateful heart to give thanks to Your name even though …

READINESS – *Encouragement and strength for spiritual battle*

- Because You have always been my deliverer, I trust You today to deliver me from …
- By Your power, let me look in triumph on the enemy of …

PSALM 55

Author   David

Category   Lament

Summary   In times of pain and fear, we can contrast our circumstances with the Lord's character, cast our burdens upon the Almighty, and trust in his sustaining mercy

B eing under the oppression of an enemy is no doubt a serious and fearful matter. But the bitter betrayal of a close friend brings a level of pain that seems unbearable. This psalm of lament, penned by King David, opens with an earnest plea to the Lord for His merciful ear to attend and respond to his complaint. This type of honest and bold calling upon the Lord saturates this song as David expresses his overwhelming terror and trembling fear (vv. 1–2, 9–11, 16–19).

Understandably, David sought an escape from his turmoil (vv. 6–8) wishing he had wings to fly away or a shelter to hide in. Instead, he boldly petitioned the Lord's intervention and judgment, asking for a divine diversion to come upon his enemies' prevalent iniquity (vv. 9–11). But the song takes a turn and gets specific and personal. The wicked oppression coming against David did not reside within an ethereal enemy but was sourced in a close companion who had betrayed his friendship. David then contrasted his palpable angst with a confident call upon the trustworthiness of the Lord in verse 16. This verse serves as a hinge to the song that swings open to a faith-evoking revelation of the Lord as the God who saves, hears ours voices, "redeems," is our souls' safety, and who humbles our enemies as the One "enthroned from of old" (vv. 16–19).

Today's readers can not only empathize with David's agony over experiencing the wound of betrayal from a close friend. But they can also consider how Christ himself encountered this type of pain and emulate how he responded. The closing lines of this psalm offer the consoling invitation that we need not bear our own trouble and heartache. Instead of running away to escape, we can release our crushing burdens to the Lord, trust in His sustaining power, and anchor our lives in His unchanging character (vv. 22–23).

PSALM 55 – GUIDE

REVERENCE – *Identify and celebrate God's praiseworthy attributes*

- Mercifully hears our prayers when we are oppressed, troubled, anguishing, fearful, and feeling betrayed – vv. 1–17, 20–21
- Attends to our prayers for safety, redeems us, and confronts our enemies – vv. 16–19
- Redeemer and safety – v. 18
- Carries our burdens, sustains us, and is our security – vv. 21–22
- Trustworthy – v. 23

Prayer Prompts

- Lord, I praise You for saving me from … especially when I was feeling …
- Thank You for the many times You have carried my burdens, especially when …
- Thank You for Your sustaining grace when I faced …
- Lord, I'm grateful I can trust You in my hardest moments because You are …

RESPONSE – *Surrender to Him and His ways*

- God, I surrender my anguish over …
- I confess I am fearful and overwhelmed about …
- Lord, I surrender the unhealthy emotions of … because of feeling betrayed by …

REQUESTS – *Ask the Spirit to guide your prayer over concerns, resources, and relationships*

- Assure me, Lord, that You hear my voice when I call out to You about …
- God, I call on You to save me from … and to redeem my soul in safety.
- Lord, even though I have been hurt and betrayed by … please redeem this relationship as I choose to trust You for protection and the power to forgive.
- I cast my burden over … on You (v. 22).
- Lord, would you sustain (name) and help them cast their burden on You.

READINESS – *Encouragement and strength for spiritual battle*

- Today, Lord, I am trusting You will cast down the enemy of …
- Help me trust in Your victory over my battle with the emotions of …

PSALM 56

Author   David

Category   Lament

Summary   David continued to be hunted by Saul and his men; attempting to escape capture, he pretended to be insane; and he lamented the ongoing threat while continuing to put his trust in the One who had always protected and sustained him

The context for this psalm is described in 1 Samuel 21:10–15, where David flees King Saul's pursuit of his life by seeking refuge among the priests of Gath. Psalm 34 corresponds to this event as well. As he did in so many of his psalms, David described those who were seeking to kill him while setting his focus on God, who protected and sustained him always.

In Psalm 56, he described those chasing him as slanderers who twisted his words, conspirators plotting his demise, lurkers who watched him closely as he sought safety. Just imagine what this must have been like, felt like, to David, who was constantly on high alert for his enemy's latest tactic to end his life. In the midst of this trouble, David revealed the reality of his fear. While looking up to the One he knew would replace his fear with faith and courage, he said, "When I am afraid, I will trust in you" (v. 3 csb). Note that he said *when*—not *if*.

David responded by pleading for God's mercy in the midst of his current troubles. His knowledge of God, personally, formed the basis for his confidence. He knew God cared and that He was intimately aware of David's current dilemma. Daivd praised God for the sure foundation of His Word and His faithfulness, asking God to intervene and disrupt his enemy's plans and purposes and to record his tearful lament as a way to defeat his enemies. God had been faithful to David, and as David fulfilled his vows to God, he was confident that God's will would continue to keep him from stumbling and would continue to bring light and life to his journey.

PSALM 56 – GUIDE

REVERENCE – *Identify and celebrate God's praiseworthy attributes*

- God is gracious and trustworthy when we are attacked and fearful – vv. 1–7, 9, 11
- God's Word is praiseworthy and true – vv. 4, 10
- He is for us and demonstrates tender and attentive care – v. 8
- Worthy of our trust, gratitude, and obedience – vv. 10–12
- The light of our lives – v. 13

> *Prayer Prompts*

- Because of Your great mercy, I am able to …
- You have been trustworthy when …
- Thank You for defending me against …
- Your Word is worthy of praise because …
- Thank You for giving me Your light when I was …

RESPONSE – *Surrender to Him and His ways*

- I confess that I am struggling with fear over …
- I admit that I need to trust Your Word and not my own emotions when …

REQUESTS – *Ask the Spirit to guide your prayer over concerns, resources, and relationships*

- Today, even in the midst of fearful circumstances, I will trust You for …
- I pray that You will assure (name) of Your nearness, even though they are shedding tears over …
- Help me to walk in obedience, with a grateful heart, even though …
- Lord, today may Your word give me light as I am walking through …

READINESS – *Encouragement and strength for spiritual battle*

- Lord, remind me that Your Word promises … especially when I feel fearful about …
- Deliver me and keep my feet from falling, especially when …

PSALM 57

Author   David
Category   Lament
Summary   From the confines of a cave, David cried out to God as King Saul continued to seek to kill him, revealing both the danger of the situation and David's absolute confidence and close relationship with God

Have you ever experienced a time in your life when it seemed like everyone was against you, trying to hurt you and malign you? Imagine. You've done nothing that would cause this kind of attack, and yet, it exists.

David wrote this poem as he sought safety from King Saul's threat by hiding in a cave, not uncommon in this part of the world (1 Sam. 22:1–5; 24:1–7). His request in the midst of this dilemma was for God's mercy. A mercy that would recognize the real danger he faced, along with God's active involvement on his behalf. His request was not for personal safety but that God would be exalted and that His glory would be known worldwide.

He described his adversaries in graphic terms. They were lions, ravenous beasts whose teeth were like spears and arrows and whose tongues spoke forth sharp words (v. 4). As if hunting wild animals, David perceived his adversaries as having "dug a pit" and "set a net" in their attempt to capture him (v. 6). This reveals the kind of danger David was facing and the immediacy of the threats. He had a decision to make. Face this threat on his own or reach out and up for help. His decision was clearly revealed as he cried out to God for His help.

David's response to this threat reveals so much about his understanding and relationship with God. He trusted in God's purpose for his life; he knew God would listen and respond to his plea, that safety exists under the shadow of God's wings (v. 1), that His love and faithfulness never end. And that He is able to reach everyone, everywhere. As a result, David's heart remained steadfast and full of the sounds of praise and thanksgiving for who God is, what He's like, and how He works. David's primary focus was that God would be exalted and glorified throughout the earth, no matter what. And he promised to keep testifying to His greatness.

PSALM 57 – GUIDE

REVERENCE – *Identify and celebrate God's praiseworthy attributes*

- Our merciful refuge in the storms of life – vv. 1
- God Most High, who fulfills His purposes for us – v. 2
- A God of steadfast love and faithfulness – vv. 3, 10
- Works to exalt His name and glory – vv. 5, 11
- Gives us steadfast and grateful hearts; fills our mouths with His praise – vv. 7–9

Prayer Prompts

- Thank You that You showed mercy and were my refuge when …
- I praise You that I have sensed the wonder of Your steadfast love even when …
- Thank You that in Your faithfulness You have always …
- Thank You that each day I can rise and praise You for …

RESPONSE – *Surrender to Him and His ways*

- Lord, I admit that I need a deeper trust in Your purposes, especially as I deal with …
- Lord, I confess that I need a greater passion for Your glory, especially about …

REQUESTS – *Ask the Spirit to guide your prayer over concerns, resources, and relationships*

- I trust in You as my refuge today as I am facing …
- Lord, give me new grace to trust Your steadfast love and faithfulness as I …
- Lord, I need a new resolve to "awake the dawn" (v. 8) each day when I am tempted to …
- Lord, I trust You to be exalted for Your glory, especially in …

READINESS – *Encouragement and strength for spiritual battle*

- Send Your help from heaven today, especially as I encounter the enemies of …
- Keep my heart steadfast in praise and gratitude, even when …

PSALM 58

Author David

Category Lament

Summary Perverted justice perverts justice; David lamented the perversions in Israel created by King Saul and his "yes men" and asked God to exact vengeance for the righteous

While in exile, I imagine David had many sleepless nights as he waited for God's goodness, faithfulness, protection, and sovereign plan to manifest itself with fulfilled promises. But David eventually learned that things have a way of working out for our good and God's glory. As I write this, I am less than a week into one of the most difficult situations I have experienced as a pastor. There is an excruciating pain deep in my soul. Yet, as I walk through it, others in even more pain are looking to people like me for strength, hope, and healing.

I have reminded myself often recently, "Mike, eventually, it will all work out for our good and God's glory." Deep in my soul I know the Lord will prove Himself good, faithful, just, and trustworthy (and you know that too). It is easy for me to trust Him when life is good, but God gets the most glory when I exercise the most trust.

Jesus hung on the cross, taking the punishment for the very sins that caused all this pain. The word *excruciating* literally means, "out of the cross." Jesus suffered an excruciating death so that "out of the cross" He could redeem excruciating moments. He will keep His promises. He will redeem this; and He can redeem whatever is causing you sleepless nights. We just have to trust His plan for our lives today.

PSALM 58 – GUIDE

REVERENCE – *Identify and celebrate God's praiseworthy attributes*

- God alone is sovereign and capable of decreeing from eternity past what is right – v. 1
- He can be trusted to judge the wickedness of men – vv. 1–9, 11
- He gives joy to and rewards the righteous, even in the midst of an evil world – vv. 10–11
- God alone is the righteous Judge – vv. 1, 11

Prayer Prompts

- I praise You as the sovereign Lord of the universe, bringing about Your decreed will, even when …
- Thank You, Lord, that even though the world around me is … You give me surpassing joy.
- I praise You that I have experienced Your reward to the righteous when I …

RESPONSE – *Surrender to Him and His ways*

- I confess that I need a greater trust in Your righteous judgment, especially when I see …
- I confess that I struggle to keep my joy when I encounter …

REQUESTS – *Ask the Spirit to guide your prayer over concerns, resources, and relationships*

- Lord, give me grace to trust Your ultimate judgment of evil so that I will not …
- Lord, give me joy today, especially when I feel overwhelmed by …
- Lord, today as I serve You faithfully in … remind me of my eternal reward.

READINESS – *Encouragement and strength for spiritual battle*

- Lord, deliver me from unrighteous anger and judgment over … knowing that You will be the eternal judge.
- Give me grace to live righteously in this evil world, especially in my reaction to …

PSALM 59

Author David

Category Lament

Summary A resilient song of trusting in God's steadfast love to deliver from all evil in order to make His rule known to the ends of the earth

I magine what it would be like to have recently been anointed the next king of a nation. You're standing, as the ultimate underdog, in the glow of defeating your people's greatest enemy. You've been given the daughter of the current king's hand in marriage, followed by the favor and friendship of the king's son. And you've begun to have songs composed about your surge of victories in battle. It seems like everything is heading in the right direction, and you're basking in God's delight and favor. Yet this trajectory of blessing is quickly interrupted by the jealous current king accompanied by a crew of men bent on your destruction and seeking to bring your newly established reputation to ruin.

Herein lies the setting of this psalm of lament. With 1 Samuel 19:11–18 as the backdrop, David's situation here was dire. He needed deliverance as a band of bloodthirsty men were hunting him down. Yet, while his enemies lay in wait, watching for the opportunity to carry out their evil plot, David chose to set his gaze on God and watched for Him to make the next move. This God of Israel is not only the Lord of hosts but also the One with the three-fold attributes of being David's strength, fortress, and steadfast love. Desperation for deliverance transitioned to a triumphant trust as David's attention to his enemies was eclipsed by the awareness of God's nearness.

The song also widens the scope of the enemy from a group of evil men to the realty of the larger battle at hand. Thus David's plea for God to punish the nations and hold them accountable was marked by a desire for God's righteous wrath to be made known – not just to the men sent by Saul but also to ends of the earth.

A crescendo of praise arises at the end of the psalm as David erupted in a resolute song extolling God once again as his strength, fortress, and steadfast love. When evil schemes sought to turn the trajectory of David's life downward, a response of resilient worship kept his focus upward and onward.

PSALM 59 – GUIDE

REVERENCE – *Identify and celebrate God's praiseworthy attributes*

- He delivers, protects, and saves us – vv. 1–2
- The Lord God of hosts, who meets us, sees us, and gives us victory – vv. 5–10
- Our strength and fortress – vv. 9, 16, 17
- Giver of steadfast love – vv. 10, 16, 17
- Our powerful shield – v. 11
- God of righteous wrath and absolute rule – v. 13
- Worthy of songs of praise – vv. 16–17

  Prayer Prompts
- Thank You that You have lovingly delivered and protected me from …
- I will sing of Your steadfast love in the morning because You have …
- Thank You that You gave me strength for the battle when …
- God, I praise You that because You are my strength and fortress I can …

RESPONSE – *Surrender to Him and His ways*

- In times of distress I confess I often run to … instead of You.
- Lord, I surrender my need to find strength in … rather than in You alone.
- God, help me to trust in You as my fortress rather than seeking security in …

REQUESTS – *Ask the Spirit to guide your prayer over concerns, resources, and relationships*

- Lord, be my strength today as I …
- Lord, bring Your deliverance/protection to (name) as they deal with …
- Lord, assure me of your steadfast love when I am feeling insecure about …

READINESS – *Encouragement and strength for spiritual battle*

- Lord my strength, I trust You to shield me today from …
- Help us trust in Your steadfast love to look in triumph on the enemy's attempt to …

PSALM 60

Author   David
Category   Lament
Summary   A cry for help in a moment of chaos

Combat veterans sometimes talk about the "fog of war" – moments on the battlefield when there's so much chaos unfolding that it's difficult to know which way to turn. That seems to be the case in Psalm 60, which the heading says was composed amid one of David's many battles and at a point where things were going so badly that it felt like God Himself was fighting against His own people. But everything changed in verse 5 when David shifted from lamenting the devastation to calling on God for deliverance: "That your beloved ones may be delivered, give salvation by your right hand and answer us!" And that's when God grabbed the microphone and emphatically declared that all of the territory in dispute belonged to Him and that, in the end, the victory and the glory for it would be His (vv. 7–12). In an instant, the fog of war cleared.

All of us experience fog-of-war moments when circumstances are so difficult that we feel like David did. And oftentimes we forget to do what David did: shift our focus away from the troubles we're facing and toward the Lord for help.

Could that be where you are today – fixated on your trial and forgetful that Jesus is in charge of it and more than able to help you through it? Remember, as a Christian, you are His "beloved" (v. 5). He will come to your aid if you ask Him to, and through Him you will eventually find victory (vv. 11–12).

PSALM 60 – GUIDE

REVERENCE – *Identify and celebrate God's praiseworthy attributes*

- He chastens those He loves – vv. 1–3
- He is a God of restoration, victory, deliverance, salvation, and answered prayer for His beloved who fear Him – vv. 1–5
- Holy, sovereign, and triumphant – vv. 6–8
- With us in battle, granting salvation and victory – vv. 9–12

    Prayer Prompts
- I thank You, Lord, that You love me enough to chasten me when I …
- I praise You that You have often restored me after I …
- I praise You that by Your right hand You have saved me from …
- Thank You for delivering me from …
- Because You are holy and sovereign, only You can …

RESPONSE – *Surrender to Him and His ways*

- I confess that in my troubles I have often fled to … rather than to You.
- I confess that I do not always fear and reverence You, especially when I …

REQUESTS – *Ask the Spirit to guide your prayer over concerns, resources, and relationships*

- Lord, today I am fleeing to You, as my banner of victory, as I am struggling with …
- Lord, assure me of Your holiness and sovereignty over … when I do not understand.
- Lord, remind me that the salvation of man is vain, and help me to trust You alone for …
- Lord, empower Your church to do valiantly, especially as we trust You for …

READINESS – *Encouragement and strength for spiritual battle*

- Lord, grant us Your surpassing help over the enemies of …
- We trust You alone to "tread down" (v. 12) our foe when we are tempted to …

PSALM 61

Author   David

Category   Confidence/Trust

Summary David recounted God's past faithfulness, using words describing the kind of protection and care God had provided over the years, and promised to keep making Him known among the people

David cried out to God from a position of weakness, frailty, and need as his heart grew faint (v. 2). He faced relentless opposition all around him. His strength was decreasing to the point where it seemed like continuing would be next to impossible. He begged for God to hear him out, to listen closely to his petitions. Maybe David thought that God might get tired of hearing from him, and so he asked for His attention. Of course, nothing could be further from the truth, as God loves His children to call out to Him at all times, whatever they might be facing or wherever they might be.

David's cry was for God's leadership in his life. Leadership that would lead him from where he was to where God is. God was David's rock, his high place, a place of strength and safety. He is a strong tower who protected David from oncoming enemies. It was in God alone that David would be protected and comforted and where he would find his hiding place. He asked God, the giver of life, to extend his own life through love and faithfulness. David desired to live in God's tent and under the shelter of His wings, like a young bird would with his mother. He longed to experience God's hospitality and care and His personal presence forever.

David concluded Psalm 61 by revealing his response to all that God had done and would do: "Then will I ever sing praise of your name and fulfill my vows day after day" (v. 8 NIV).

PSALM 61 – GUIDE

REVERENCE – *Identify and celebrate God's praiseworthy attributes*

- God hears our prayers no matter how we feel or where we are – v. 1
- Our eternal rock of refuge and strong tower – vv. 2–4
- The heritage and sustainer of those who fear Him – vv. 5–6
- Watching over us in steadfast love and faithfulness – v. 7
- Worthy of our praise and daily obedience – v. 8

Prayer Prompts

- Thank You for hearing me when ...
- I praise You that You were my refuge and strength when ...
- You have been faithful when I was ...
- Your steadfast love assures me when I feel ...
- I praise You because Your name is ...

RESPONSE – *Surrender to Him and His ways*

- I admit that I sometimes seek security in ... rather than in You, my true rock.
- I confess that I struggle in my commitments to You, especially in the area of ...

REQUESTS – *Ask the Spirit to guide your prayer over concerns, resources, and relationships*

- Because You hear, I cry out to You for ...
- Give me the security that only You can provide when I am ...
- I pray that the next generation will know that You are ... because of the testimony of my life.
- Remind me that You sustain my life when I am prone to trust in ...
- Assure me that Your steadfast love and faithfulness are watching over me today when ...

READINESS – *Encouragement and strength for spiritual battle*

- Today, I will trust You as my strong tower when the enemy tries to ...
- When my heart is faint, give me renewed trust in Your strength, especially when I am tempted to ...

PSALM 62

Author   David
Category   Trust
Summary   God is ready to speak to us, but we must choose to listen

How long can you sit still before getting restless? Our world today is anything but conducive to moments of quiet, peaceful contemplation. But as Christians, sometimes that is what our souls need most!

Look at how David began this Psalm: "For God alone my soul waits in silence; from him comes my salvation." Yet, just two verses later, his thoughts had shifted to enemies who were seeking to do him harm. So in v. 5 he said it again: "For God alone, O my soul, wait in silence, for my hope is from him." Having forced himself to once again give the Lord his full attention, his view of those enemies was radically transformed (vv. 8–10).

There is no Scriptural guarantee that God will speak directly to you if you try to sit quietly in His presence for a couple of minutes. But sitting quietly in His presence for a couple of minutes (or more!) can certainly prepare you to hear from Him, whether through His Word, a Holy Spirit prompting, or a truth about Himself that He brings to your mind. Look closely at vv. 11–12 and you'll see that's what happened with David.

Take some time right now and try it yourself: sit down, sit still, ask the Spirit to quiet your heart, and *wait in silence for God alone*. Who knows what He might want to tell you today?

PSALM 62 – GUIDE

REVERENCE – *Identify and celebrate God's praiseworthy attributes*

- He alone is our salvation, rock, and fortress when we are feeling insecure – vv. 1–2, 6–7
- Our hope – v. 5
- Our trustworthy God who welcomes the outpouring of our hearts – v. 8
- A God of power, steadfast love, and ultimate judgment – vv. 11–12

Prayer Prompts

- I praise You that You have been my salvation when …
- Thank You; because You are my rock and fortress, I do not have to be shaken when …
- I praise You that You are my true hope when I encounter …
- Because You are trustworthy, I know I can pour out my heart over …
- Because power belongs to You, you are able to …

RESPONSE – *Surrender to Him and His ways*

- I admit that it is hard for me to be silent and wait on You alone, especially when …
- I confess that I sometimes tend to trust … rather than waiting on You.

REQUESTS – *Ask the Spirit to guide your prayer over concerns, resources, and relationships*

- Lord, help me to wait on You alone in silence as I deal with …
- Because You are my rock and my salvation, I trust You for the burden of …
- Be a fortress today for (name) so they will not be shaken by …
- Because power belongs to You, give me faith to know that You can …

READINESS – *Encouragement and strength for spiritual battle*

- Because You are my mighty rock and fortress, I will trust You to protect me from the enemy when he tries to …
- Fix my eyes on You today when my heart is tempted to …

PSALM 63

Author David
Category Confidence
Summary David's prayer of desperation for the presence of God

Have you ever been driven to desperation? Are you finding yourself desperate today? Perhaps you are desperate for a job or a friend or a special someone to love. Maybe it is physical healing or mental and emotional healing that you desperately need. In Psalm 63, we find David driven to a place of desperation. Literally, his enemy had chased him into the desert wilderness, where he was probably desperate for water and food – quite possibly near death. He was desperate for protection, desperate to be home, desperate to be restored in relationships. "Desperate times call for desperate measures." What do you do when you find yourself in desperate times?

In the midst of extreme desperation, David cried out to God, not in hopeless despair but in confident praise and adoration. David began by affirming his covenant belonging to God and his devotion to seeking God (v. 1). The main point of the psalm is the truth that only God can satisfy the most desperate longings of the soul (vv. 1–8). Yes, he needed food, water, and shelter; he needed life's basics. However, David saw the bigger picture. In fact, David's physical needs reminded him of his even more important spiritual need. That is, the very presence of God. To be in the presence of our loving God is more satisfying than any other experience life could give us (v. 3). So, even in desperate times, David set his heart on knowing and trusting God as the One who sustained and satisfied him (vv. 5–8).

Evil men among the Israelites who were rebelling against God and wanting to kill him drove David to flee into the wilderness. Even so, David's confidence was in God. Anyone who chooses to trust God can share in this confidence and experience satisfaction, even in desperate times (vv. 9–11).

PSALM 63 – GUIDE

REVERENCE – *Identify and celebrate God's praiseworthy attributes*

- Our God who is worthy to be sought with earnest thirst and desire – v. 1
- A God of power, glory, steadfast love – better than life – vv.2–3
- Worthy of our lifelong praise, blessing, and worship – vv. 3–4
- Giver of satisfaction, joy, help, strength – vv. 5–8

Prayer Prompts

- My God, I worship You because You have quenched my soul's thirst for …
- Thank You for revealing Your power and glory to me when …
- I praise You because Your love is better than …
- Your help gave me great joy when …

RESPONSE – *Surrender to Him and His ways*

- Father, I admit that I have sometimes sought satisfaction in …
- I confess that at night, my mind is distracted by … rather than meditating on You.

REQUESTS – *Ask the Spirit to guide your prayer over concerns, resources, and relationships*

- Lord, give me grace to thirst for You more than …
- Father, I need Your right hand to uphold me as I …
- Give me grace to praise You with joyful lips even when …
- God, please help (name) discover satisfaction in you.

READINESS – *Encouragement and strength for spiritual battle*

- God, when the enemy seeks to tempt me with lies about … silence him through my mediation on Your Word!
- God, we know that in the end you will have victory over …

PSALM 64

Author   David
Category   Lament
Summary   Even when evil runs rampant, God will have the last word

One of the greatest gifts the Psalms offer us is their unvarnished realism. They confront the world as it is, not as we wish it to be, and this psalm of David is a prime example. The underlying sentiment of vv. 1–6 is one that each of us knows well. We see wickedness at every turn, and what's worse, it seems like those doing it always get away with it. Like David we cry, "That's not right! It shouldn't be allowed! This isn't how the world is supposed to be!" Sound familiar?

But then, in verse 7, we meet two of the most beautiful words in Scripture: *"But God."* David reminded us that the Lord is sovereign and He doesn't miss a thing. He will ensure that, by His righteousness, every injustice will be overcome and that, in the end, everyone will bow down and give Him glory (v. 9).

What troubles are burdening your heart today? David's counsel here in Psalm 64 was to lay them before God in prayer one at a time. Then immediately follow each one with a prayerful, *"But God"* affirmation that it really is under His control and that His purposes will ultimately prevail. That's what it means to "be glad in the LORD and take refuge in Him" (v. 10 NASB), and doing so has a funny way of making your problems seem not quite as big as they were before taking them to the Lord in prayer.

Psalm 64 – Guide

REVERENCE – *Identify and celebrate God's praiseworthy attributes*

- He hears, preserves, and hides us when the enemy attacks – vv. 1–6
- He fights our battles for us – vv. 7–8
- He works on our behalf so others will fear Him and recognize His hand at work – v. 9
- He makes us righteous, gives us joy, and is our faithful refuge – v. 10

   Prayer Prompts
- I praise You, Lord, that You heard my prayer and preserved my life when …
- Even though the enemy plots secretly against us, You are able to …
- Thank You that You worked in my life powerfully when … so that others saw Your hand at work.
- I rejoice in You because You were my refuge when I …

RESPONSE – *Surrender to Him and His ways*

- Lord, I confess that I have trusted in … rather than You when I have been under attack.
- Lord, I admit that I have tried to fight my battle with … in my own strength.

REQUESTS – *Ask the Spirit to guide your prayer over concerns, resources, and relationships*

- Lord, I am trusting You to preserve me today as I struggle with …
- Lord, I want people to see Your hand at work in my life, especially as I trust You for …
- I pray that (name) will find great joy as they trust You to be their refuge in the midst of …
- Help me to have joy and live uprightly before You, especially as I deal with …

READINESS – *Encouragement and strength for spiritual battle*

- Lord, I trust You to fight for me in my battle with … so that others will fear You.
- Lord, give me confidence that You will be my refuge when the enemies of the gospel try to …

PSALM 65

Author   David
Category   Praise
Summary God atones for our sins so He can bless us with His presence and provision

What do I consider the greatest blessings in my life? Is it my spouse, my children or grandchildren, my financial stability, or my vocational success? Psalm 65 is a celebrative song of praise reminding Israel of how God atoned for their sin so that He could grant them, as His righteous followers, abundant agricultural blessings. David used this festive time of harvest celebration to remind Israel an important lesson: we are to love *the Blesser* more than the blessing.

In the midst of receiving the physical bounty of God's provision, Israel was not to lose sight that the preeminent blessing was being chosen by the Lord, to be brought near to Him, to dwell in His presence. "Blessed is the one you choose and bring near, to dwell in your courts! We shall be satisfied with the goodness of your house, the holiness of your temple!" (v. 4). David admonished Israel to be satisfied with the goodness and holiness of being in God's presence because he knew from experience how easy it is to be distracted by the blessings and miss *the Blesser*!

In the midst of receiving forgiveness of sins and the abundant blessings that follow, I ask: "What truly satisfies me?" Do I consider being in the holiness of God's presence as the greatest blessing of my life, and does His presence satisfy the deepest longings of my soul?

PSALM 65 – GUIDE

REVERENCE – *Identify and celebrate God's praiseworthy attributes*

- God hears and is approachable – v. 2
- God atones for sin and saves – vv. 3, 5
- He satisfies, He is joy – vv. 4, 12–13
- He is awesome, righteous, and all-powerful – vv. 5–6
- God visits, enriches, waters, and blesses the earth – v. 9

Prayer Prompts
- God, You are due praise because …
- I am in awe of You because …
- Lord, I praise You because …
- God, being in Your presence is incomparably better than …

RESPONSE – *Surrender to Him and His ways*

- God, iniquities often prevail against me. Thank You for atoning for my sin of …
- I confess I pursue satisfaction in … but You alone satisfy my soul.
- Lord, because You have chosen me to be *in* Your presence, I will choose to be satisfied *with* Your presence.
- God, I am truly grateful for Your abundant provision, but thank You even more for bringing me near to dwell in Your courts when …

REQUESTS – *Ask the Spirit to guide your prayer over concerns, resources, and relationships*

- God, because You hear my prayers, I come to You asking You to …
- As You visit the earth with rain, please visit (name) and provide their need of …
- Lord, by awesome deeds You answer with righteousness, so please provide (name's) righteous need of …

READINESS – *Encouragement and strength for spiritual battle*

- God, because You sustain all creation, please sustain me as I go into the harvest field …
- God, as I go today, gird me with Your joy so I can sing and shout for joy with all creation.

PSALM 66

Author   David
Category Praise/Joy
Summary   Celebration of God's deliverance of His people

C hristians are truly blessed by God. Just think of all the things He has done for you personally.

David, who may well have been the author of this psalm, loved to think back and recount the many blessings God had bestowed upon His people.

In Psalm 66 the author reminded us of the Red Sea crossing. Pharaoh and his army were chasing the Israelites, when suddenly they had no place to go. The sea was ahead of them; Pharaoh and his army were behind them. God caused a strong wind to blow upon the water until it stood up in a heap! The Israelites then crossed the sea on dry ground. Pharaoh and his army pursued the Israelites right into the dry ground of the sea. But then God caused the wind to cease and the sea stormed back upon Pharaoh and his army until all the Egyptians were drowned.

God is pure and holy, and when we approach Him, we must come before Him in purity and holiness. We do not have that purity in and of ourselves, but we receive the purity of Christ when we fall before Him in confession and repentance. God, then, seeing the purity of Christ instead of our sins, answers our prayers. Hallelujah!

PSALM 66 – GUIDE

REVERENCE – *Identify and celebrate God's praiseworthy attributes*

- His name is glorious – v. 2
- He is awesome, great, and powerful – v. 3
- Worthy of worship and does amazing works – vv. 4–5
- He rules, is mighty and eternal – v. 7
- He keeps and protects – vv. 9–12
- Worthy of blessing because He hears and responds – v. 19

Prayer Prompts

- I praise You, O Lord, for Your great work of ... How awesome are Your works!
- Thank You for the assurance that You are ruling over ...
- Thank You for attending to the voice of my prayer, especially when ...
- I sing praises to Your name, O Lord, because You are ...

RESPONSE – *Surrender to Him and His ways*

- Let me not forget the lessons You taught me when You were refining me, especially the lesson of ...
- I too often regard the wickedness of ... in my heart. Please forgive me.

REQUESTS – *Ask the Spirit to guide your prayer over concerns, resources, and relationships*

- Knowing that You keep us in this life and do not let our steps slip, I pray for (name) today, that You will ...
- Lord, let me always be mindful of the promises I have made to You, especially ... Give me grace to obey.
- Lord, because of the greatness of Your name, I know I can trust You today for ...

READINESS – *Encouragement and strength for spiritual battle*

- Because You keep watch over the nations, I trust You to watch over me, especially when I face ...
- When I am tempted to cherish the sin of ... turn my eyes to You and deliver by Your power.

PSALM 67

Author   Unknown

Category   Praise

Summary   A joyful song of the multitude of ways God extends His blessing to and through His people and out to all the nations of the earth.

There is a tendency for certain words to get so overused that they either become anemic to our hearts and minds or forgotten altogether. One word that seems overused in our Christian vocabulary is the word *bless* or *blessing*.

Biblically speaking, a blessing is something that is graciously given for the benefit of someone else. Yet a blessing can also be directed upward toward God to convey heartfelt praise and adoration. Psalm 67, one of God's divinely inspired songs, brings back into view the amazing reality of what it means to bless or to be blessed. In just seven short verses, this psalm reveals at least five realities of what God's blessing entails. It also serves to reclaim the word *bless* from flippancy and turn it to fervency.

The psalm actually begins with a benediction, which brings into focus the blessing of God's presence. No doubt this opening line is a restatement of the well-known Aaronic blessing found in Numbers 6:24–26. What the opening line of Psalm 67 and the benediction in Numbers 6 make clear is that God's blessing is primarily about who He is and secondarily about what He does or gives. God's blessing arises out of His gracious character, which then extends to His merciful dealings with humanity. The emphasis here on God's face redirects the reality of blessing from a self-focus to a Godward focus.

Next, the psalmist declared a straightforward connection to the purpose of God's presence among His chosen people. The direction of God's blessing in this psalm is clear. It is not meant merely for our inward enjoyment but for outward multiplication. The blessing of God's saving power was never meant to stop with Israel, but it was intended to flow through Israel and out to all the nations.

God's blessing is also revealed within the context of communal praise. The psalmist repeated an exuberant chorus of joyful praise twice in this song (vv. 3, 5), once again directing us back to a Godward focus. It is an immense blessing to praise and celebrate who God is, and it is a privilege we will enjoy for all eternity.

Lastly, the song concisely reveals the ways God's blessing comes to us in the forms of protection (v. 4) and provision (v. 6). The closing verse reminds us that all of God's blessings are meant to point us back to God as *the Blesser* and to walk in the fear of the Lord.

PSALM 67 – GUIDE

REVERENCE – *Identify and celebrate God's praiseworthy attributes*

- God is gracious and the source of all blessing – vv. 1, 6–7
- A powerful savior, worthy of the praise of all people – vv. 2–3, 5
- Source of gladness and joy, righteous judge, guide of the nations – v. 4
- A faithful provider, to be feared and revered – vv. 6–7

    Prayer Prompts
- I praise You for the blessing of ...
- Lord, we are glad and sing for joy because You are ...
- Lord, we join all the peoples in praise of You because ...

RESPONSE – *Surrender to Him and His ways*

- Lord, I confess that I have not made Your way known when ...
- God, I repent of hoarding Your blessing of ... and not allowing it to flow through me to others.

REQUESTS – *Ask the Spirit to guide your prayer over concerns, resources, and relationships*

- God, because of Your grace, please bring Your blessing to ...
- Because You guide the nations, I trust You to guide (name) as they ...
- Lord, cause Your saving power to be made known to ...
- Lord, we pray for Your justice and guidance (v. 4) in ...
- Lord, I pray for the work of the gospel in the nation of ... that Your people will join in praise of You (vv. 3, 5)!

READINESS – *Encouragement and strength for spiritual battle*

- I pray that Your saving power to the nations will go forth mightily to overcome Satan's strongholds in the nation of ...
- Lord, as we join You in taking the gospel to the nations, protect us from the enemy's efforts to ...

PSALM 68

Author David
Category Praise
Summary Extravagant praise to God Almighty, who is sovereign and good

D avid had a great God! This song is full of joyful praises to the Champion of the people of Israel. The psalm is a testament to God's conquering power over every enemy His people face. David left us with a rich catalog of some of God's names and characteristics, along with the kinds of people He delights to help.

This is our God ...

- I am God, Father, and Protector.
- I am a holy Deliverer, merciful Leader, and good Provider.
- I am almighty, eternal, and omnipotent.
- I am the Risen One – Benefactor, Savior, Conqueror, and King.
- I am a mighty voice, strong and awesome.
- "I AM WHO I AM" (Ex. 3:14).

These are His people ...

- The fatherless, widows, the lonely, the captives and imprisoned
- The weary, the poor, the needy
- Those who are humble and lowly
- The sick and dying
- The least, the unlikely, the weak, and the helpless
- "Come to me, all who labor and are heavy laden, and I will give you rest" (Matt. 11:28).

This is our response ....

- *I believe* ... Jesus Christ has conquered every enemy of my soul.
- *I sing* ... joyful praises to Him who alone is worthy.
- *I declare* ... that God will deliver all who sincerely call upon His name.
- "Go home to your friends and tell them how much the Lord has done for you, and how he has had mercy on you" (Mark 5:19).

Psalm 68 – Guide

REVERENCE – *Identify and celebrate God's praiseworthy attributes*

- He confronts and defeats His enemies – vv. 1–2
- He gives gladness, joy, and cause to praise to the righteous – vv. 3–4
- A holy protector and provider to His children – vv. 5–6
- Leads His people with abundance, restoration, goodness, truth, and victory – vv. 7–18
- Sustains, saves, and delivers – vv. 19–23
- Our God, King and source of blessing – vv. 24–27
- Powerful, mighty, majestic, and awesome in this power of strength – vv. 32–36

Prayer Prompts

- I praise You, Lord, that You have given me divine victory over …
- Thank You, Lord, that Your joy always transcends …
- I sing praise to You because Your name is …
- Thank You that You led me through difficult days when …
- My God and King, I bless You because …

RESPONSE – *Surrender to Him and His ways*

- Lord, I know I often forfeit the joy of righteous choices when I …
- Lord, I confess that I've sometimes felt like I am in parched lands, especially when I disobey You by …

REQUESTS – *Ask the Spirit to guide your prayer over concerns, resources, and relationships*

- Lord, would You act as the "Father of the fatherless" (v. 5) on behalf of (name) as they …
- Because You are a protector of widows, I pray for (name), that You will …
- In Your goodness, I pray that You will restore …
- God of salvation, I pray that You will deliver (name) from …

READINESS – *Encouragement and strength for spiritual battle*

- Because You have delivered Your people in the past, I trust You to deliver me from …
- Through the mighty voice of Your Word, give us power and strength, especially when the enemy tries to …

PSALM 69

Author   David
Category   Confidence/Trust
Summary   God will come to the aid of the desperate in their time of trouble

In Psalm 69 David was up to his neck in trouble while he was waiting for God to answer his prayers. He graphically described his state: *I'm sinking , I'm drowning, I'm overwhelmed, I'm worn out* (vv. 1–3). *My enemies are so many I can't even number them* (v. 4). *God seems to be hiding when I need Him most* (v. 17). Even his own family had forsaken him (v. 8), and a sympathetic friend couldn't be found (v. 20). Ever been there? Alone and overwhelmed by life's storms?

In September 2004, I was hit with three storms in one week. First Hurricane Frances devastated much of the east coast of Florida where I live. Two days later I learned that my mother had died. Next came the tearful call from my thirty-year-old daughter, Christy, informing me that she had just been diagnosed with stage 4 breast cancer. I responded by saying, "We are going to pray like crazy for your healing, but remember, the enemy will use this to slander God's character, so you must stand on the truth of God's Word as well as your own experience of His goodness." Christy would pass into the presence of the Lord twenty-two months later.

I remember pouring out my heart to the Lord in prayer, questioning. "Why?" and "How long, O Lord?" Then I sensed the Lord asking me two questions:

- *"When you dedicated her to Me, did you mean it?"*
- *"Who does she really belong to?"*

I responded, "Yes, Lord, I meant it," and "Yes, she belongs to You." The issue was settled. I believed God's choice would be best. Peace immediately filled my heart.

Our prayers were not answered as we hoped, but God faithfully upheld us in our grief. So whatever crisis or trial you may be facing right now, be encouraged by David's closing exhortation: "May the hearts of those who look to God for help be refreshed"(v. 32 GW).

Jesus is Victor! Psalm 69 begins in a pit and ends in that beautiful city inhabited by God ... and those who love Him.

PSALM 69 – GUIDE

REVERENCE – *Identify and celebrate God's praiseworthy attributes*

- A Savior who knows our despair and meets us at our point of deepest need – vv. 1–12, 33
- A Savior of steadfast love, faithfulness, and deliverance – vv. 13–15, 35
- Full of goodness and mercy; draws near to us and redeems – vv. 16–18
- Knows our distress and judges His enemies on our behalf – vv. 19–29
- Worthy of praise, magnification, and thanksgiving – vv. 30–31
- Giver of gladness and reviver of spirit – v. 32

   Prayer Prompts
- I praise You that in the abundance of Your steadfast love, You heard my desperate prayer when ...
- I praise and thank You because, throughout my life, You have ...
- Lord, I love Your name because ...

RESPONSE – *Surrender to Him and His ways*

- Lord, I know that those who love Your name could be brought to shame through me if I ... Give me a spirit of repentance and the grace of Your holiness.
- Lord, I confess that I cannot deliver myself from ... Help me trust the power of your salvation.

REQUESTS – *Ask the Spirit to guide your prayer over concerns, resources, and relationships*

- Lord, I am overwhelmed by ... Save me by Your power so that ...
- Help me, Lord. I am deeply troubled by ...
- Father, will You strengthen (name) as they face ...
- Lord, You know that I am weary now because ... Give me new grace to trust you for ...

READINESS – *Encouragement and strength for spiritual battle*

- Even when others attack me by ... give me the assurance of Your steadfast love.
- Lord, deliver me from the enemy of ... as I put my trust in You today.

PSALM 70

Author   David
Category   Lament
Summary   An urgent prayer for God to quickly come to save David, which would give joy to those who trust in God.

E ach of us has been at the end of our rope, at a time in our lives where we had no other place to turn except to God. And in that time when we cry out, we cry that God would come quickly. David's request for God's rapid response opens and closes Psalm 70.

David's adversaries were seeking to shame and publicly humiliate him (v. 3). In an Eastern culture where honor and shame are defining values, to be publicly humiliated is a significant threat. David's prayer was that those who were trying to put him to shame would be shamed themselves; those who sought to ruin him would experience their own disgrace. In a sense, David was asking God to quickly turn the tables on his accusers so they would get what they were dishing out.

Though David was in difficult circumstances, he still exalted God. While his enemies wanted to shame him and seek his ruin, David responded with this: "Let God be exalted" so they can "rejoice and be glad" (v. 4 WEB).

Before God, David acknowledged his vulnerability (v. 5). While he was not financially poor and needy, he, nonetheless, acknowledged his complete dependence upon God. David realized, as we should as well, that our deliverance comes from God, not from our wisdom, our actions, or our control. So when we're at the end of our ropes, we can, as David did, cry out, "You are my help and my deliver; O LORD, do not delay!"

PSALM 70 – GUIDE

REVERENCE – *Identify and celebrate God's praiseworthy attributes.*

- The One who saves, helps, vindicates, and protects – vv. 1–3
- A great Savior, the source of joy and gladness for those who seek Him – v. 4
- The exalted helper and deliverer – v. 5

Prayer Prompts
- I praise You that You hear my cry when …
- Thank You for delivering me when …
- I praise You that I can rejoice and be glad in You because …

RESPONSE – *Surrender to Him and His ways*

- When people seek to shame me, help me to turn to You instead of …
- Help me to acknowledge that I am poor and needy when …

REQUESTS – *Ask the Spirit to guide your prayer over concerns, resources, and relationships*

- Give me joy in the Lord in the midst of …
- May those who seek to shame me know Your grace, so that …
- Come quickly to help me in …

READINESS – *Encouragement and strength for spiritual battle*

- Be my help and deliverer today for …
- Deliver (name) from the shame of …

PSALM 71

Author   David

Category   Lament

Summary   An aging David's acknowledgement that God had been and would continue to be his refuge

P salm 71 is a continuation of Psalm 70. They are meant to be read together. Psalm 70 was David's cry to God. In Psalm 71, David requested that God would be his refuge (vv. 1, 3, 5, 7). In crying out, David was putting his hope in God for his deliverance, that God would rescue, deliver, and save him.

David acknowledged in his old age (v. 5) that his hope and confidence in God had sustained him since birth (v. 6). Though some people perceived David's suffering throughout his lifetime as God's displeasure in him (v. 7), he acknowledged that God Himself remained his refuge when the troubles of life were overwhelming. This was evident when David's enemies continued to try to shame him (Ps. 70:2–3) and justify their behavior against him believing that God had forsaken him (Ps. 71:11). David continued to lean into God for deliverance (vv. 12–13).

Once again he expressed confidence and hope in God. David would tell of this hope even in his old age, declaring it to the next generation (vv. 14–18, 24) so that they may know God's righteousness (v. 19), faithfulness (vv. 20, 22), and redemption (v. 23).

David confessed a lifetime of God's grace and deliverance, from birth (v. 6) to grey hair (v. 18). And even when he was weak with old age, he would attest to and declare the strength and power of God, his refuge and strength.

PSALM 71 – GUIDE

REVERENCE – *Identify and celebrate God's praiseworthy attributes*

- God is our refuge – vv. 1, 3, 5, 7
- God rescues and delivers us from our enemies – vv. 2–3
- He is righteous and our source of hope – vv. 14–16, 19, 24
- God is faithful, the One who redeems – v. 22

Prayer Prompts

- I praise You that You are my confidence even if …
- Thank You for being my rock and fortress when …
- I praise You for Your faithfulness to me when …
- Because I have hope, I praise You more and more for …

RESPONSE – *Surrender to Him and His ways*

- When things seem to be going against me, help me to turn to You and not to …
- Lord, I confess that when I hit hard times, I seek refuge in … rather than in You.

REQUESTS – *Ask the Spirit to guide your prayer over concerns, resources, and relationships*

- Deliver me from the "hand of the wicked" (v. 4) when …
- Help me declare Your marvelous deeds to the next generation(vv. 17–18) as I commit myself to …
- When I am advancing in age and in deteriorating health, give me continued strength to glorify You (v. 18), especially when …

READINESS – *Encouragement and strength for spiritual battle*

- Although I am troubled about … may it be evident to all that You are my refuge.
- Lord, even when I face … empower me to tell of Your righteousness to …

PSALM 72

Author   Solomon

Category Royal

Summary A prayer for Solomon's reign, that the nations would experience God's blessing through him

W hen a new person is in charge, whether it is a small business owner, middle management, CEO, or US president, it should be our prayer that they fulfill God's calling to be a person who demonstrates the characteristics of justice, righteousness, mercy, and compassion.

Psalm 72 is written for the coronation of a king, as it reflects the ideals of a perfect king. The ideal ruler would bring the fruits of justice, righteousness, hope, security, and well-being to his kingdom. It is then that the world would see and praise God.

A quick reading of the Old Testament kings shows that none of them lived up to these ideals fully. Yet God promised that a king in the line of David would rule forever. It is in Jesus, the promised Messiah and King, that this expectation is fulfilled.

In the reign and rule of King Jesus, it is God alone who will endure (v. 5) and bring prosperity and righteousness and justice (vv. 2–3) to His Kingdom. It is Jesus who cares for the marginalized, the needy, and the afflicted (v. 4). And it is ultimately before King Jesus that all nations will bow down (v. 11; Phil. 2:11; Rev. 7:9), as His rule and reign will last forever (v. 5, 17).

PSALM 72 – GUIDE

REVERENCE – *Identify and celebrate God's praiseworthy attributes*

- He is just and righteous – vv. 1, 2, 7
- Defends the marginalized and cares for the needy – vv. 4, 12–14
- Endures forever and rules over all – vv. 5, 8, 11
- Brings blessing to the world – v. 17
- Does marvelous deeds – v. 18

Prayer Prompts

- I praise You that You are the perfect ruler over …
- Thank You that You delivered me in my time of need when …
- I bless You, Lord, for Your wondrous deeds, especially …

RESPONSE – *Surrender to Him and His ways*

- Lord, I need a deeper fear of You. Forgive me when I am drawn to fear … instead.
- Lord, I have often overlooked the needy in my community. Make my heart more compassionate and responsive by …

REQUESTS – *Ask the Spirit to guide your prayer over concerns, resources, and relationships*

- God, may Your reign and rule be recognized through me as I …
- Help me to be a witness to the glory of King Jesus, especially to …
- Lord, I need a greater commitment to the needy and oppressed. So today, I commit to …
- Lord, I need Your blessing in order to be a blessing to others. So today I trust You to use me to …

READINESS – *Encouragement and strength for spiritual battle*

- Lord, help me walk in Your righteousness today, especially when …
- Let me reflect the glory of Your name each day, even when …

APPENDIX A
PSALMS BY CATEGORY

Wisdom (Psalms 43, 49)

Psalms of wisdom hold in tension the two contrasting themes of righteousness and wickedness. They are meant to further teach us that the way of wickedness is marked by foolishness leading to ruin while the way of righteousness exemplifies wisdom bringing peace and flourishing (e.g. Ps. 52).

Prophecy (Psalms 50)

A select few psalms resonate the prophetic focus of calling God's people to repentance in order to reestablish covenantal faithfulness. Often the main voice of these unique psalms is God Himself (e.g. Ps. 50).

Lament (Psalms 42, 44, 51 - 53, 55 - 60, 64, 70, 71)

Outside of praise, lament is most dominant theme of Psalms. Lament psalms are honest and passionate expressions of the pain caused by living in a broken and fallen world. They bring the whole person into an authentic encounter with God who is strong enough to bear our burdens, powerful enough to answer our bold requests, and good enough to trust with our suffering (e.g. Ps. 42).

Praise/Joy (Psalms 47, 48, 65 - 68)

These psalms creatively expound upon and exalt the character and attributes of the Lord. They are meant to orient us towards a unified seeking of God's face in order to be satisfied in His presence. Often these songs reveal how praising God is not to be confined to a single group of people, but rather to be multiplied and spread to reach all nations (e.g. Ps. 67).

Thanksgiving

While closely tied with psalms of praise, which focus on exalting God's character, psalms of thanksgiving bring attention to the way the Lord works in our lives. Often recalling past actions and answered prayers, these psalms are saturated with exuberant gratitude and filled with a zeal to spread the knowledge of the Lord's work to all people (e.g. Ps. 30).

Confidence/Trust   (Psalms 46, 54, 61 – 63, 69)

These songs instill a deep assurance within our souls that God can be trusted. Despite difficult circumstances, God's faithfulness serves as our confidence and equips us to lovingly obey as we wait upon Him to fulfill His Word (e.g. Ps. 62).

Royal   (Psalms 45, 72)

Even though these songs often overlap with other categories, they carry a special emphasis on God as King who has chosen to establish His reign through human agents. Sometimes they are also called Messianic psalms as they bring to remembrance the Davidic covenant which ultimately points to Christ as God's anointed Ruler and King (e.g. Ps. 72).

APPENDIX B

HISTORICAL CONTEXT AND STRUCTURE OF THE PSALMS

Psalms is a masterfully composed anthology of ancient Israel's songs and prayers that covers almost a millennium of history. Within the 150 chapters, there exists a beautifully complex variety of poetic genres including hymns of joy, lament, thanksgiving, and psalms of confidence, remembrance, wisdom, and kingship. The arrangement of the various themes seems intentionally random, making it difficult on one hand to interpret any given psalm in its original context, but on the other hand making the book of Psalms applicable to a universal audience. Given the broad scope of the composition, it seems best to assume that the historical background of the Psalms is the history of the nation of Israel. This assessment informs and guides the theological implications of the Psalms and, thus, would lead any reader to broadly claim that the theology of the Psalms is the theology of the whole Old Testament.

The early church fathers thought the Psalms were uniquely the microcosm of the Bible. Athanasius (c. 296–373) likens them to the variety within a botanical garden, while Basil the Great (c. 329–79) describes them as a great storehouse. For most of the history of the church they were the layman's major Biblical source of faith and devotion.[4]

The structure of the Psalms is broken down into a collection of five books (which is why *Praying the Psalms* will be released as five separate volumes). While scholars continue to delve into this curious structural component, one leading explanation is that the Psalms are meant to correspond to and reflect the first five books of the Old Testament, also known as the Pentateuch or Torah. In other words, there is an intentional inter-textual relationship between the Torah and Psalms that ought to shape and inform our reading and understanding. Additionally, this relationship seems to remind the original readers that Psalms held equal authority and relevance to the Torah as divinely inspired Scripture. Jewish tradition viewed the Psalms as a second Pentateuch (Torah) and as an echo of the first. So much so that a rabbinic

---

4 Bruce K. Waltke, James M. Houston, and Erika Moore, *The Psalms as Christian Worship: A Historical Commentary* (Grand Rapids, MI: William B. Eerdmans Publishing Company, 2010), 117.

commentary of Psalm 1 states "as Moses gave five books of laws to Israel, so David gave five "books" of Psalms to Israel."[5]

This structural dynamic further comes to light as the beginning psalm in each of the five "books" seems to transition emphasis and themes that correspond to the Pentateuch. And keeping in step with the overall theme of Psalms, each of the five "books" concludes with a doxology of praise. Consistent with a particular literary device of Hebrew poetry, one scholar relates the five "books" of the Psalms to the Pentateuch in a chiastic, or inverted order.[6] Thus, the Pentateuch ends where the Psalms begin and the Psalms end where the Pentateuch begins. In order to visualize this powerful dynamic, the following chart seeks to summarize the key relational components of the Psalms and Pentateuch:[7]

Pentateuch	Psalms	Theme	Praise
Deuteronomy	Psalms 1-41 (Book 1)	The importance of obedience to God's law.	"Blessed be the LORD, the God of Israel, from everlasting to everlasting! Amen and Amen." ~Psalm 41:13
Numbers	Psalms 42-72 (Book 2)	The trials of God's people and hope for a future restoration.	"Blessed be His glorious Name forever; may the whole earth be filled with His glory! Amen and Amen! ~Psalm 72:19
Leviticus	Psalms 73-89 (Book 3)	The distinct community of God's people marked by faith and holiness.	"Blessed be the LORD forever! Amen and Amen." ~Psalm 89:52

---

5 William G. Braude, *The Midrash on the Psalms,* vol 1(New Haven: Yale University Press, 1959), 5.

6 John S. Vassar, *Recalling a Story Once Told: An Intertextual Reading of the Psalter and Pentateuch* (Macon, GA: Mercer University Press, 2007), 9–10)..

7 The themes section of the chart are influenced and summarized from Vassar, *Recalling a Story Once Told.*

Pentateuch	Psalms	Theme	Praise
Exodus	Psalms 90-106 (Book 4)	The LORD's liberation of Israel and the wilderness wanderings of the people of God.	"Blessed be the LORD, the God of Israel, from everlasting to everlasting! And let all the people say, "Amen!" Praise the LORD!" ~Psalm 106:48
Genesis	Psalms 107-150 (Book 5)	The LORD's creative and saving intervention in the lives of the faithful.	"Let everything that has breath praise the LORD! Praise the LORD!" ~Psalm 150:6

While the chart above simply provides a concise overview, further study of the Psalms alongside the Pentateuch will promote their striking connection with ever increasing depth and clarity. Yet what is most vital about the relationship between the Psalms and Pentateuch is not how they reference each other, but rather what they both point the reader towards.

It is significant to remember that of all the Old Testament Scriptures that are quoted in the New Testament, Psalms rises to the top of the list just above Isaiah. In their commentary on the Psalms, Bruce Waltke and James Houston note that of the 283 direct quotations of the Old Testament in the New Testament, 116 or 41% of them are from the Psalms.[8] They go on to observe that Jesus alludes to the Psalms over fifty times and then draw the powerful conclusion that "when New Testament writers explicitly cite Psalms, which are written in small letters with reference to David, they write in capital letters with reference to Christ.[9]"

Both the Psalms and Pentateuch, like all of Scripture, ultimately have a cross-worn path and are best interpreted and applied Christologically. A powerful scene of the resurrected Christ in Luke 24 conveys this dynamic with striking clarity when Jesus proclaims to two puzzled disciples, "O foolish ones, and slow of heart to believe all that the prophets have spoken! Was it not necessary that the Christ should suffer these things and enter into his glory?" (vv. 25–26). And beginning with Moses and all the Prophets, He interpreted to them in *all the Scriptures the things concerning Himself*" (Luke 24:25-27 *emphasis added*). Just moments later, this "Bible study" with Jesus resulted in the disciple's profound response when

---

8 Waltke, Houston, and Moore, *The Psalms as Christian Worship*, 110.

9 Waltke, Houston, and Moore, 110.

they exclaimed, "Did not our hearts burn within us while He talked to us on the road, while He opened to us the Scriptures?" (Luke 24:32). For these two disciples, ignorance was overcome by intimacy as prayer ("He talked to us on the road") and the word ("He opened to us the Scriptures") converged and empowered them to testify to what God had done (cf. Acts 6:4). Jesus reiterates this vital truth of all Scripture being fulfilled in Himself one more time before He commissions all of His disciples to proclaim the gospel, "Then He said to them, 'These are My words that I spoke to you while I was still with you, that everything written about Me in the Law of Moses and the Prophets and the Psalms must be fulfilled'" (Luke 24:44). All of the correlating themes of the Pentateuch and Psalms, then, are fulfilled in the person and work of Christ, which elicits a heartfelt response of praise.

As one writer put it, "If the Bible's narrative materials relate what God has done and the prophetic literature reports what God has said, the Psalms present the response of the people to the acts and words of God."[108] So as we journey through *Praying the Psalms,* may we, with burning hearts, respond in the same way David did in Psalm 40:5 when he declared, "You have multiplied, O LORD, my God, your wondrous deeds and your thoughts toward us; none can compare with you! I will proclaim and tell of them, yet they are more than can be told."

10 Limburg, J. (1992). Psalms, Book of. In D. N. Freedman (Ed.), *The Anchor Yale Bible Dictionary* (Vol. 5, p. 522). New York: Doubleday.

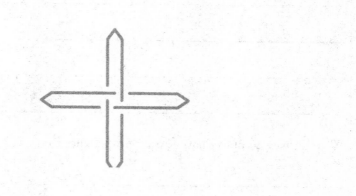

MY JOURNEY – REFLECTIONS

Date:

Scriptures:

What I have learned about God, myself, others, and circumstances?

_____

_____

_____

_____

_____

What answers to prayer have I seen or experienced?

_____

_____

_____

_____

_____

_____

MY JOURNEY – REFLECTIONS

Date:

Scriptures:

What I have learned about God, myself, others, and circumstances?

_____

_____

_____

_____

_____

_____

What answers to prayer have I seen or experienced?

_____

_____

_____

_____

_____

_____

_____

MY JOURNEY – REFLECTIONS

Date:

Scriptures:

What I have learned about God, myself, others, and circumstances?

_____

_____

_____

_____

_____

_____

What answers to prayer have I seen or experienced?

_____

_____

_____

_____

_____

_____

_____

MY JOURNEY – REFLECTIONS

Date:

Scriptures:

What I have learned about God, myself, others, and circumstances?

_____

_____

_____

_____

_____

_____

What answers to prayer have I seen or experienced?

_____

_____

_____

_____

_____

_____

_____

MY JOURNEY – REFLECTIONS

Date:

Scriptures:

What I have learned about God, myself, others, and circumstances?

_____

_____

_____

_____

_____

_____

What answers to prayer have I seen or experienced?

_____

_____

_____

_____

_____

_____

_____

MY JOURNEY – REFLECTIONS

Date:

Scriptures:

What I have learned about God, myself, others, and circumstances?

_____

_____

_____

_____

_____

_____

What answers to prayer have I seen or experienced?

_____

_____

_____

_____

_____

_____

_____

MY JOURNEY – REFLECTIONS

Date:

Scriptures:

What I have learned about God, myself, others, and circumstances?

_____

_____

_____

_____

_____

_____

What answers to prayer have I seen or experienced?

_____

_____

_____

_____

_____

_____

MY JOURNEY – REFLECTIONS

Date:

Scriptures:

What I have learned about God, myself, others, and circumstances?

_____

_____

_____

_____

_____

_____

What answers to prayer have I seen or experienced?

_____

_____

_____

_____

_____

_____

_____

MY JOURNEY – REFLECTIONS

Date:

Scriptures:

What I have learned about God, myself, others, and circumstances?

_____

_____

_____

_____

_____

What answers to prayer have I seen or experienced?

_____

_____

_____

_____

_____

_____

_____

MY JOURNEY – REFLECTIONS

Date:

Scriptures:

What I have learned about God, myself, others, and circumstances?

_____

_____

_____

_____

_____

_____

What answers to prayer have I seen or experienced?

_____

_____

_____

_____

_____

_____

_____

MY JOURNEY – REFLECTIONS

Date:

Scriptures:

What I have learned about God, myself, others, and circumstances?

_____

_____

_____

_____

_____

_____

What answers to prayer have I seen or experienced?

_____

_____

_____

_____

_____

_____

_____

MY JOURNEY – REFLECTIONS

Date:

Scriptures:

What I have learned about God, myself, others, and circumstances?

_____

_____

_____

_____

_____

_____

_____

What answers to prayer have I seen or experienced?

_____

_____

_____

_____

_____

_____

_____

My Journey – Reflections

Date:

Scriptures:

What I have learned about God, myself, others, and circumstances?

_____

_____

_____

_____

_____

_____

What answers to prayer have I seen or experienced?

_____

_____

_____

_____

_____

_____

_____

_____

MY JOURNEY – REFLECTIONS

Date:

Scriptures:

What I have learned about God, myself, others, and circumstances?

_____

_____

_____

_____

_____

_____

_____

What answers to prayer have I seen or experienced?

_____

_____

_____

_____

_____

_____

_____

_____

My Journey – Reflections

Date:

Scriptures:

What I have learned about God, myself, others, and circumstances?

_____

_____

_____

_____

_____

_____

What answers to prayer have I seen or experienced?

_____

_____

_____

_____

_____

_____

_____

MY JOURNEY – REFLECTIONS

Date:

Scriptures:

What I have learned about God, myself, others, and circumstances?

_____

_____

_____

_____

_____

_____

What answers to prayer have I seen or experienced?

_____

_____

_____

_____

_____

_____

_____

MY JOURNEY – REFLECTIONS

Date:

Scriptures:

What I have learned about God, myself, others, and circumstances?

_____

_____

_____

_____

_____

_____

What answers to prayer have I seen or experienced?

_____

_____

_____

_____

_____

_____

_____

MY JOURNEY – REFLECTIONS

Date:

Scriptures:

What I have learned about God, myself, others, and circumstances?

_____

_____

_____

_____

_____

_____

What answers to prayer have I seen or experienced?

_____

_____

_____

_____

_____

_____

_____

MY JOURNEY – REFLECTIONS

Date:

Scriptures:

What I have learned about God, myself, others, and circumstances?

_____

_____

_____

_____

_____

_____

What answers to prayer have I seen or experienced?

_____

_____

_____

_____

_____

_____

_____

MY JOURNEY – REFLECTIONS

Date:

Scriptures:

What I have learned about God, myself, others, and circumstances?

_____

_____

_____

_____

_____

_____

What answers to prayer have I seen or experienced?

_____

_____

_____

_____

_____

_____

_____

MY JOURNEY – REFLECTIONS

Date:

Scriptures:

What I have learned about God, myself, others, and circumstances?

_____

_____

_____

_____

_____

_____

What answers to prayer have I seen or experienced?

_____

_____

_____

_____

_____

_____

_____

MY JOURNEY – REFLECTIONS

Date:

Scriptures:

What I have learned about God, myself, others, and circumstances?

_____

_____

_____

_____

_____

What answers to prayer have I seen or experienced?

_____

_____

_____

_____

_____

_____

_____

MY JOURNEY – REFLECTIONS

Date:

Scriptures:

What I have learned about God, myself, others, and circumstances?

_____

_____

_____

_____

_____

_____

What answers to prayer have I seen or experienced?

_____

_____

_____

_____

_____

_____

_____

MY JOURNEY – REFLECTIONS

Date:

Scriptures:

What I have learned about God, myself, others, and circumstances?

_____

_____

_____

_____

_____

What answers to prayer have I seen or experienced?

_____

_____

_____

_____

_____

_____

_____

MY JOURNEY – REFLECTIONS

Date:

Scriptures:

What I have learned about God, myself, others, and circumstances?

_____

_____

_____

_____

_____

_____

What answers to prayer have I seen or experienced?

_____

_____

_____

_____

_____

_____

_____

MY JOURNEY – REFLECTIONS

Date:

Scriptures:

What I have learned about God, myself, others, and circumstances?

_____

_____

_____

_____

_____

_____

What answers to prayer have I seen or experienced?

_____

_____

_____

_____

_____

_____

_____

MY JOURNEY – REFLECTIONS

Date:

Scriptures:

What I have learned about God, myself, others, and circumstances?

_____

_____

_____

_____

_____

_____

What answers to prayer have I seen or experienced?

_____

_____

_____

_____

_____

_____

_____

MY JOURNEY – REFLECTIONS

Date:

Scriptures:

What I have learned about God, myself, others, and circumstances?

_____

_____

_____

_____

_____

_____

What answers to prayer have I seen or experienced?

_____

_____

_____

_____

_____

_____

_____

 **STRATEGIC RENEWAL**

Our greatest need is Jesus Christ living through a revived church.

Strategic Renewal's vision is to see praying Christians supporting praying pastors who lead praying churches into supernatural gospel impact. Every revival in history that resulted in a spiritual awakening in society always began in movements of extraordinary prayer.

Strategic Renewal is igniting the heart of the church through practical resources, extraordinary events, and equipping pastors for a renewed emphasis on Scripture-Fed, Spirit-Led, Worship-Based Prayer.

www.strategicrenewal.com

THE 6:4 FELLOWSHIP
Pastors Committed to Prayer and the Ministry of the Word

The 6:4 Fellowship, a ministry of *Strategic Renewal*, is developed by pastors for pastors to encourage one another to a resolute commitment to "prayer and the ministry of the Word" – the roots of revival. The ministry reawakens pastors to the clear ministry priority found in Acts 6:4. Putting "first things first" positions churches to experience stunning outcomes – the fruits of revival – similar to those encountered by early believers as described in Acts 6:7.

As a diverse and international community, 6:4 *calls* pastors to this preeminent devotion. The ministry practically *coaches* leaders toward deeper *conviction, competency*, and *confidence* in "prayer and the ministry of the Word." Relationally The Fellowship *connects* these pastors to one another in an authentic, worldwide, prayer-fueled *community*.

A major focus of the ministry is to model and train others in *Scripture-fed, Spirit-led, Worship-based prayer*, following the pattern of "The Lord's Prayer" (Matthew 6:9-13).

www.64fellowship.com